Sunset

ideas for great
kitchens

By Jane Horn and the Editors of Sunset Books

Menlo Park, California

Sunset Books

VICE PRESIDENT, GENERAL MANAGER: Richard A. Smeby
VICE PRESIDENT, EDITORIAL DIRECTOR: Bob Doyle
PRODUCTION DIRECTOR: Lory Day
DIRECTOR OF OPERATIONS: Rosann Sutherland
MARKETING MANAGER: Linda Barker
ART DIRECTOR: Vasken Guiragossian
SPECIAL SALES: Brad Moses

Staff for This Book

MANAGING EDITOR: Sally W. Smith
COPY EDITOR/INDEXER: Phyllis Elving
PHOTO DIRECTOR/STYLIST: JoAnn Masaoka Van Atta
ART DIRECTOR: Vasken Guiragossian
ILLUSTRATOR: Beverley Bozarth Colgan
PRINCIPAL PHOTOGRAPHER: Jamie Hadley
PAGE PRODUCTION: Janie Farn
PRODUCTION SPECIALIST: Linda Bouchard
PREPRESS COORDINATOR: Eligio Hernandez
PROOFREADER: David Sweet

10 9 8 7 6 5 4 3 2 1
First Printing June 2006
Copyright © 2006, Sunset Publishing
Corporation, Menlo Park, CA 94025.
Third edition. All rights reserved,
including the right of reproduction
in whole or in part in any form.

ISBN-13: 978-0-376-01238-8
ISBN-10: 0-376-01238-2
Library of Congress Control
Number: 2006921540.
Printed in the United States of America.

For additional copies of *Ideas for Great Kitchens* or
any other Sunset book visit us at www.sunsetbooks.com or
call us at 1-800-526-5111.

Photography credits
Cover main image: Beatriz Coll; top left: Thomas J. Story;
top middle: Dominique Vorillon; top right: Margot Hartford.
Cover design by Vasken Guiragossian.
Page 1: Heather Reid.
Above: Courtesy of Blum.
Right: Tria Giovan.
Facing page top: Jay Graham; bottom: Muffy Kibbey.
Page 5: Margot Hartford.

Home Cooking

Everyone wants a kitchen—the heart of the home—that's functional, stylish, and airy. Perhaps that's why kitchen remodels are the superstars of home renovation, inspiring a panoply of options for everything from appliances to cabinets to countertops. Planning a space that holds its own for the long term can be daunting. Let this newly revised entry in Sunset's "Ideas for Great…" series help nail it all down. You'll find hundreds of photos illustrating the latest designs and materials. Color palettes for selected kitchens help you choose combinations that will work for you. First page to last, it's a solid introduction to kitchen planning as practiced by the pros.

Many kitchen professionals, businesses, and homeowners helped us by providing advice and information, or by opening their doors to our photo crew. We'd especially like to thank the following individuals and firms, all of California: Lisa Joyce of Lisa Joyce Architecture, Piedmont; Peter Kyle of Woodworks Construction and Design, Berkeley; Brad Milenbach of Friedmans Appliance, Pleasant Hill; Douglas H. Aaseby, O.D., of Lights of Rafael, San Rafael; Sherri Buffa of Capstone Cabinetry and Design, Inc., Oakland; Belmont Hardware, Belmont; Kitchen Matrix, San Francisco; La Vita è Bella, Inc./Scavolini, San Francisco.

For the names of photographers and designers whose work is featured in this book, turn to pages 142–143.

On the
MENU

THESE DAYS, A KITCHEN MUST WORK HARD for the cook, look great, and also be a hangout—and not just at mealtimes. The trend is toward open, multipurpose rooms that flow into adjoining living areas. In response, new kitchens tend to be bigger (although you can live large in less square footage by making some simple, smart changes). What's filling all that space? You'll see a sophisticated mix of materials and styles, fine cabinet finishes, expansive islands, built-in appliances, and innovative storage and media components.

You want a kitchen that's a true reflection of how you live. This book will guide you to the decisions that are right for you. The first section, "Ideas and Inspiration," is a photo-packed gallery. Then "How to Do It" details the nitty-gritty of kitchen design. Together, they'll help you cook up the kitchen of your dreams.

Ideas and
INSPIRATION

IS TODAY'S KITCHEN about far more than breakfast, lunch, and dinner? Of course it is, as the photos on the following pages make clear. The spaces presented here may differ in style, size, and layout, but their common thread is how well they all adapt to busy modern lifestyles. There's plenty of food for thought for your own new kitchen, from smart strategies for storage, food prep, lighting, entertaining, and even lounging to ideas for elegant finishing touches.

Great
Kitchen Spaces

EVERYONE SEEMS TO END UP in the kitchen these days. What's the attraction? Maybe the magnet is amenities like breakfast banquettes, dining tables, message centers, home offices, and comfortable sitting areas. Or could it be kitchen islands that serve as space dividers, storage lockers, wet bars, and eating counters as well as repositories for school projects and business reports?

Today's kitchen is no longer the simple space of your grandmother's day, when mealtimes were set and one cook did it all. Expanded in both size and function, it has become the heart of the home, a place for meals, gatherings, and family projects.

In the following pages, we offer a photographic tour of kitchens that work at every level. As you browse, think about your own space and needs. Do you want your kitchen to be open or closed? An open plan is the more popular option right now, but it does have its drawbacks: work areas must be organized carefully, noise can be a problem, and privacy is an issue (do you mind messy pots and dirty dishes in full view?). A closed kitchen offers solitude for cooks who prefer to work uninterrupted and unseen, but it also limits socializing during preparation and cleanup.

Left: Unmistakably Old World in style, this kitchen glows with rich color. The upper cabinet and custom range hood are both finished in a sunny yellow that really pops against the brick-red wall.

Are you contemplating a cozy nook where you can grab your morning coffee and toast before heading off to work? Do you envision a large island, finished like a piece of fine furniture, for serving hors d'oeuvres or a buffet dinner to a crowd? We'll show you these setups and more.

Also depicted are kitchens that accommodate a gamut of activities by organizing them into zones—for baking, for cleanup, for homework or hanging out. These flexible, defined spaces allow both the cook (or cooks) and other individuals to be engaged in separate activities, yet remain in friendly proximity. It's a trend that is inspiring many kitchen designers to break away from the traditional sink-stove-refrigerator work triangle layout.

An efficient, hardworking floor plan is the jumping-off point for any successful kitchen design. Yours may stay within the current "footprint" of the room or annex adjacent space to achieve a more functional layout and more open living area. You'll find inspiration here in both classic and innovative examples, along with ideas for living large in a small kitchen.

Above right: Brightly colored walls and striped fabric draw attention back to the breakfast area, making this kitchen, reconfigured but not enlarged, feel bigger than it used to.

Lower right: The visual bulk of this island is minimized by elevating the eating bar at one end. A sandblasted glass top opens up the space, as does the slender brushed-metal support pole.

Right: Booth seating, a standard feature in diners, makes good use of a small, formerly empty kitchen corner. Bare windows create a light-filled place to sit, while Craftsman details add character.

Below: More than just a cozy nook, this breakfast bay is activity central. Here, homework gets done, games are played, and the family has dinner together every evening.

Above: Rustic touches are everywhere in this expansive kitchen, from the simple wrought-iron chandelier to rush-seat dining chairs—and lots of wood.

Left: This contemporary dining nook makes use of sleek metal and plenty of pizzazz. A "V" pattern is a subtle design element repeated on the table base and seat backs, pulling it all together.

Above and left: Formerly dark and cramped, this traditional kitchen–family room is now bright and spacious. The full wall that divided two rooms came down, replaced by a half wall that encourages easy interaction between the spaces. The column is load-bearing. In the sitting area (far left), barn-red chairs, country checks, antique rugs, and tile floor create an ambience of casual elegance. The sunny niche at one end of the kitchen (near left) was originally completely filled by a window; for much-needed storage, the lower portion was replaced with cabinetry.

Right: Island living suits even the family dog in this serene kitchen. The countertops are fabricated of quartz, a durable engineered stone.

Below: This open kitchen needs to hold its own, design-wise, with the rest of the surrounding space. Concealing considerable storage, the sleek Euro-style cabinets are both handsome and functional.

Above: A baking area topped with Italian marble, ideal for working with pastry, extends from the main work island. Rolling out dough is less tiring on a lower work surface.

Left and below: This neo-Victorian kitchen is warm and inviting, with walls the color of watermelon, crisp white trim, and cherry cabinetry. The floor is resilient cork. A folding stepstool pulls out from under a cabinet to provide a boost.

GREEN *Kitchens*

How does sustainability—conserving resources—translate to kitchens? It can mean everything from energy-efficient construction and appliances to salvaged, renewable, or locally sourced materials—and, of course, regular recycling of waste and trash. Environmentally friendly also means health-conscious design: protecting indoor air quality by using products and finishes that don't emit toxic fumes. What it doesn't mean is any particular decor or architectural style; you can still follow personal taste when it comes to how your kitchen looks.

- **Appliances.** To earn the Energy Star rating, appliances must operate below the minimum federal standards for energy consumption. For example, Energy Star refrigerators must use at least 15% less energy than federal standards require. Look for dishwashers and washing machines with shorter washing and drying cycles to save water and power.

- **Cabinets.** Consider cabinetry constructed from formaldehyde-free particleboard or wheatboard (made from straw waste bound with nontoxic adhesives), bamboo, certified lumber (meets environmental standards set by the nonprofit Forest Stewardship Council), or formaldehyde-free laminate.

- **Countertops.** Look for certified lumber, concrete, lightweight concrete with recycled glass (terrazzo), Richlite (paper content), or tile.

- **Flooring.** Choose bamboo, lyptus (a newly introduced, quick-growing hybrid wood that resembles hardwood), concrete, cork, high-pressure laminate, linoleum, recycled or certified lumber, coconut palm, or tile.

- **Lighting.** Fluorescent lights use less energy than incandescents and last far longer (see "Fluorescent Facts," page 63).

- **Recycling.** Install easy-to-access bins for recyclables. Compost your produce waste.

- **Wall finishes.** Green choices include paints rated low- or no-VOC (volatile organic compounds), recycled-glass tiles, and wallpaper made of natural, renewable, or recyclable material.

- **Windows.** Low-e, double-glazed, and argon-filled windows and glass doors offer maximum energy efficiency.

Eco-friendly choices shown below include a quartz countertop, recycled tile backsplash, wheatboard cabinets, and bamboo flooring. For energy-saving tips, visit the U.S. Department of Energy's Energy Star program Web site (www.energystar.gov).

Above: Deep crown molding copied from the dining room, granite countertops, and a new white oak floor transform what was once a bare-bones kitchen. White cabinets, trim, and ceiling capture the light, while cherry surfaces add warmth along the right side of the room.

Right: A playful mix of materials gives this contemporary kitchen personality plus. Cabinets of laminated plywood are simply styled to showcase accents of brushed aluminum and swaths of color.

Left: The sleek cabinets in this glamorous European-style kitchen were custom built and finished to order at the factory, simplifying installation onsite. The long, brushed-metal pulls are both handsome and easy to grasp.

Left: This troughlike porcelain farmhouse sink, part of the kitchen shown below, is the command center for post-meal cleanup. Open shelves put dishware and utensils within reach.

Left: Inspired by its rural setting, this home melds straight-from-the-farm materials with modern finishes. In the open kitchen, board-and-batten siding and simple cabinets contrast with a stainless-steel island and restaurant-style appliances.

Above: This elegant kitchen is the result of carefully chosen materials, including a glass-tile backsplash and brushed-nickel hardware, paired with a harmonious palette of muted blue-green cabinets and countertops of gray honed granite and yellow-green concrete.

Left: A freestanding work table at counter height doubles as an eating bar. An island of some form is a necessity in such a large space in order to divide the room, reducing steps.

Below: In a kitchen corner, this family computer center features cabinets of maple and a countertop of quartz, a new surfacing material.

Facing page, inset: This elegant workstation was designed to blend into the kitchen without giving it an "office" feel, thanks to cabinets and a built-in desk made to resemble freestanding furniture.

Right: A compact message center squeezed into one corner of the kitchen is where the family calendar, phone book, cookbooks, laptop, and other often-used essentials are kept.

Above: For many kids, the kitchen is a favored spot for homework. Occupying a central spot, this computer station is accessible to the whole family.

Right: Sliding doors reveal a mini-office and hide a pantry, a washer and dryer, and a water heater, reducing visual clutter and providing a great place for items requiring deep storage.

What's *Your Style?*

FOCUS ON THE FEELING YOU WANT your kitchen to convey. Contemporary or traditional? Boldly colorful or warm and cozy? You may already have a style in mind, but before you commit to a scheme, think about its staying power. Will the kitchen you are installing today scream its age long before you're ready to remodel? Try to distinguish between looks that are trendy and those that will endure.

Defining details

A style inspired by your home's architecture is always a good idea. But rarely are kitchen decorating schemes completely consistent representations of particular styles. More often, it's all about the details. Hybrids abound—traditional looks with modern materials, for example. Painted white or natural wood cabinets are timeless, as are hardwood floors. And if the kitchen is open to adjoining spaces, it should match or at least complement the overall look. Here are seven popular styles for kitchens and some of the details that typically define them.

◀**Contemporary.** Bright, airy, and uncluttered, with clean-lined, unbroken surfaces; glossy finishes (for minimalist spaces); streamlined fixtures; simple recessed-panel or slab cabinets; metal and glass accents; brushed-metal hardware; black, white, or stainless-steel appliances; recessed lighting and pared-down pendant or track lighting; bare windows.

Cottage. Informal and cozy, with a modest sense of scale; natural wood and light colors; unfitted furniture-style or beadboard cabinets; distressed finishes; open shelving including plate racks and rails; unmatched hardware; farmhouse sinks; wood, rustic tile, or linoleum floors; vintage accessories.

Country. Light woods, often with a bleached, distressed, painted, or natural finish; darker hardwoods such as pecan and cherry; paneled and arched cabinets; farmhouse sinks; honed (not glossy) work surfaces; exposed wood beams; stone, tile, or wide-plank wood floors; antique and handcrafted accessories.

▼**Craftsman.** An emphasis on natural, handcrafted materials; strong angular forms; warm-toned woods; straightforward flat-panel cabinets; traditional forged or wrought-iron hardware; stone countertops; vintage light fixtures; art glass; subtle colors.

▶**Mediterranean.** Warm, sunny colors; painted or natural finishes; fanciful hardware; stone countertops; exposed wood beams; arches; decorative plaster and/or tile vent hoods and range alcoves; tile backsplashes and floors; handcrafted accessories.

◄Retro. Vintage appliances (either actual restored models or heirloom-style modern ones); subway-tile backsplashes; tile or laminate countertops; farmhouse sinks; pharmacy-style pulls; glass knobs and doorknobs; plate rails; wood floors or resilient tile flooring laid in a checkerboard pattern.

▼Traditional. Somewhat formal; raised-panel, flush-inset, and furniture-style cabinetry; wainscoting; darker hardwoods; rich finishes; ornate hardware; traditional fixtures; carved detailing on crown molding, vent hoods, and cabinet panels; stone countertops; chandelier light fixtures; upholstered seating; window coverings.

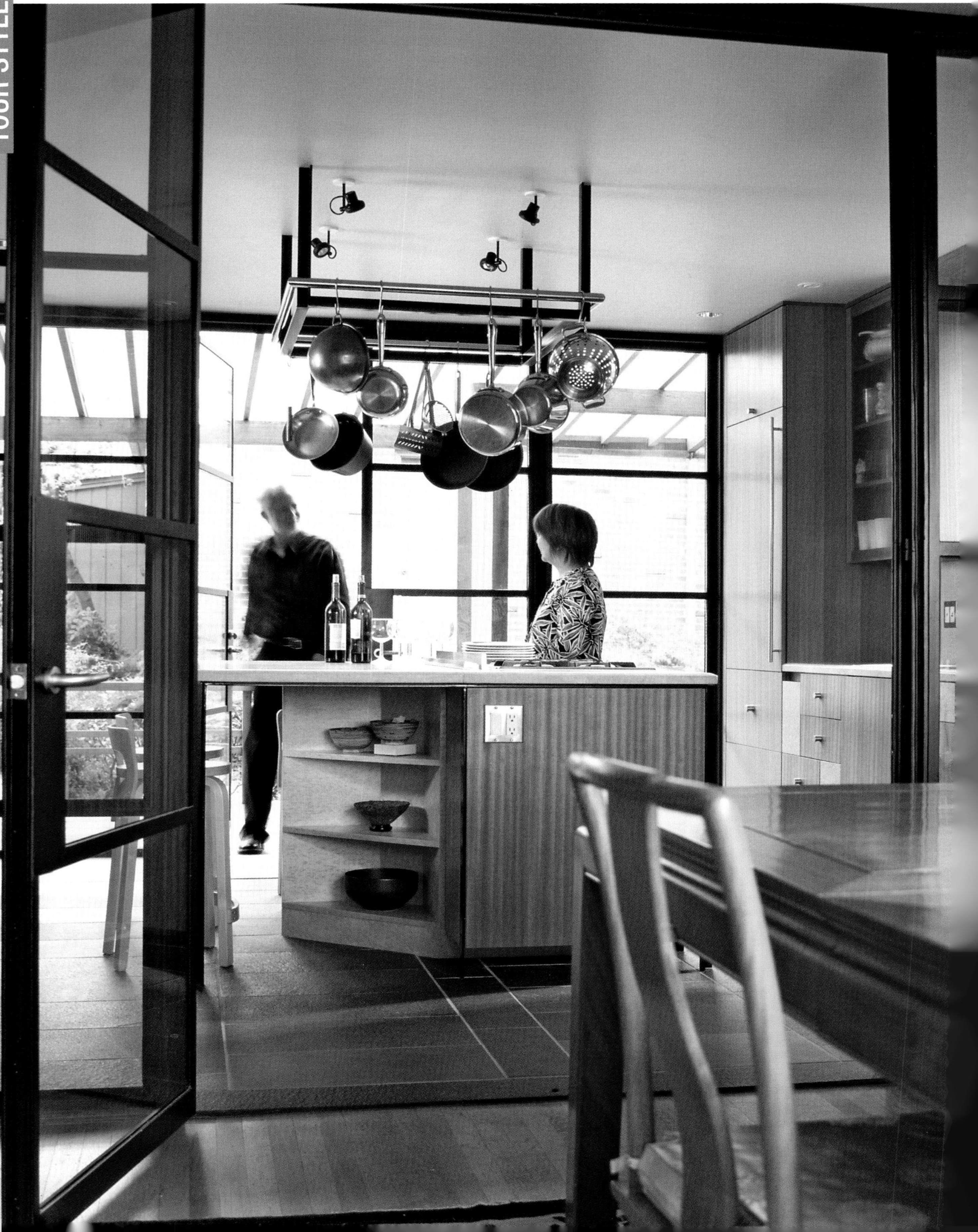

Below: Tall cabinets made of ribbon-stripe mahogany fill the side walls of the kitchen also pictured at left. Their shallow depth is perfect for a pantry.

Left and above: Transparent glass walls connect this contemporary kitchen with the adjacent dining room and backyard deck. Swapping part of a brick interior wall for bold, elegant steel-and-glass doors lets the cook socialize without interrupting food preparation.

Above: A touch of paint in the form of a faux urn gives an island cabinet the artistic appeal of a Tuscan fresco. Warm, earthy colors reinforce the Mediterranean mood.

Below: A beamed ceiling is not what you'd expect in a streamlined kitchen like this one, yet the linear arrangement looks quite modern.

The marriage of Victorian charm and modern convenience works well in this updated farmhouse kitchen. Retro details like glossy subway tiles and a beadboard ceiling emphasize the kitchen's vintage character.

Left: A mix of materials and finishes gives this contemporary kitchen real eye appeal. The counter is polished granite that reflects the light, while frame-and-panel cabinets are lightly glazed to bring out door detail.

Right: Despite the sleek, up-to-the-minute restaurant-style range, this kitchen is to the manor born. The ornately embellished vent hood, supported by equally decorative corbels, is a real showpiece.

Below: Rich, dark wood cabinets contrast strikingly with clear glass, a white farmhouse sink, and white walls. The deep-hued frames of the windows and doors continue the Craftsman style.

Storage *Strategies*

SUFFICIENT STORAGE IS ALWAYS AN ISSUE when you are designing a kitchen. Any remodeling plan needs to take advantage of every square foot of available space. One popular solution: pantries are back to help shoulder the kitchen storage overload. You'll also get some good ideas from the practical yet inventive approaches shown on the following pages.

Fortunately, there's an organizing system to suit every size and style of kitchen. Interior shelving options improve the efficiency of your cabinets and make it easier to get to what's inside. Lazy Susans and swing-out shelves revitalize typically unusable corners. Roll-out shelves, flatware dividers, fitted plate and pot holders, and recycling pullouts all make your cabinets work harder for you.

How to maximize storage without sacrificing style? Plate racks and open shelving can turn everyday tableware into decorative accessories. Freestanding hutches and armoires give the kitchen a furnished look while increasing its storage space. Sleek banks of built-in floor-to-ceiling shelving—either left open or enclosed behind doors—are a popular trend as homeowners trade traditional overhead cabinets for more windows and natural light.

Left: Many cabinet manufacturers offer pantry units as accessories. These narrow pullouts make full use of cabinet depth and are conveniently accessible from both sides.

PANTRY
Primer

The centralized food storage areas of your grand-mother's day are still a good idea. In fact, the old-fashioned pantry is making a comeback—updated to handle busy modern lifestyles that encourage bulk buying and reliance on special appliances and tools to shortcut food prep. The good news: any size kitchen can outfit a pantry.

Ready-made pantries are available in almost any size and shape, from narrow cabinets to elegant armoires adapted for kitchen storage. Convert an underutilized space in your kitchen, or create a pantry in a nearby closet outside the kitchen. Incorporate pull-out pantry units, popular for their ease of access, into new cabinetry. A floor-to-ceiling shelf unit that pulls all the way out is handy if you have the room for one; most cabinet manufacturers offer them. Retrofit existing cabinets with ready-to-install systems available at home centers or storage specialty shops.

Know the size of the largest item you'll be storing—that family-size cereal box, your heavy-duty electric mixer, or the bin in which you keep flour—before configuring any storage system. Bring all the measurements with you to the showroom.

Right: To display a collection of baskets and Italian pottery, the homeowner vetoed a door on the pantry. The interior lights up each time the threshold is crossed, thanks to a motion sensor.

Right: With added shelving, an existing closet is easily converted into a pantry. These are simple planks obtainable at lumberyards or home centers; other options are ready-to-install units from home centers and storage specialty shops.

Facing page: On the surface, the storage in this run of cabinets seems about as deep as a jar of jam. But a full pantry hides behind doors that mimic adjoining cabinetry when they are closed.

Above: Pivoting wire shelving rather than fixed shelves gives this custom pantry easier access and greater flexibility. Shallow units hung on the inside of cabinet doors are perfect for seasonings and condiments.

Right: Two large pantry units slide into a service wall devoted to storing dishes, crystal, and favorite accessories for entertaining.

Below: A freestanding storage cabinet in a dark wood finish delineates one end of this European-style galley kitchen. Although it resembles an antique armoire, it was actually built for the room. A hanging cabinet that resembles an old-fashioned plate rack adds personality to the kitchen.

Above: These cabinets utilize every inch of available storage space, thanks to clever interior components that pull out, swing out, or swivel. Two solutions for hard-to-reach corners are a lazy Susan (top left) and a swivel-and-glide shelf system (top right). A skinny sliding shelf unit creates a handy stoveside pantry (bottom left), while a recycling unit holds four separate bins (bottom right).

Left and below: The large island that dominates this kitchen earns its generous square footage: it provides storage and a spot for the microwave, a perch for casual dining or conversation, and a surface for entertaining buffet style. The kitchen base cabinets step down in height as they extend into the family-room area (left), visually separating the spaces and breaking up a long cabinet run.

Above: Glass-front doors, open shelving, and hooks for mugs prevent upper storage in this kitchen from looking top heavy. Grid-like compartments maintain order in the hanging cabinet.

Right: It's the details that give these cabinets the look of freestanding furniture: contrasting finishes and surface materials, varied heights, multiple storage built-ins, and feet rather than the usual bases.

41

Left: These elegant cabinets have details you'd find in fine antique furniture, like glass doors with Gothic-style muntins and decorative brackets. The flush-inset drawers are another hallmark of quality construction.

Above: Cantilevered open shelving and closed cabinets below combine to create beautiful and efficient storage. The spare modern lines and watery palette provide a neutral backdrop for the owner's colorful ceramics.

Left: A wall of translucent cabinets keeps this kitchen/breakfast area feeling open while providing plenty of storage. Tableware stored within view makes for easy, one-stop table setting at mealtime.

Above and right: Custom drawer storage holds dishes in place and spices in order. Shallow shelving on the dining-room side of the kitchen island turns tableware into an attractive gallery display, adding visual interest to an otherwise solid wall of cabinetry.

Below: Pull-out baskets in this island give easy access to staples like bread loaves or foods that need air circulation, like onions and potatoes.

In this streamlined modern kitchen, open shelves in the marble-topped island put everyday glassware and dinnerware front and center.

45

Above: A wood divider between the dining area and the kitchen is a buffet/bookcase on one side and a backsplash for the sink on the other. The two niches that flank the faucet add handy storage space.

Left: Otherwise wasted corner space is put to good use with a two-tiered lazy Susan storage unit. The shelves swing out, bringing items within easy reach.

Above: A third bank of storage fits neatly between upper and lower cabinets. Here, small appliances hide behind lift-up doors, eliminating countertop clutter.

Right: Here are two options for drawers: movable pegs that accommodate dishes of different shapes and sizes (left), and rods that keep contents from sliding around (right).

Working *Assets*

APPLIANCES ARE NO LONGER the boring drones of kitchens past. Manufacturers have drafted the best design talent to punch up their style as well as to improve their function. And there's an appliance sized for every floor plan, from condominium-compact to restaurant-substantial. You'll find eye-catching refrigerators with curvy profiles and sleek wall ovens with architectural handles.

On the other hand, some appliances have all but disappeared behind custom cabinet panels and faux drawers. They've become quieter, too. Better insulation has hushed dishwasher noise to the point that an "on" light is often the only way to know if a machine is running. Refrigerator "hum" is now a whisper, and ventilation fans have lowered their decibels.

Stainless-steel finishes remain popular. Those who prefer a less commercial look can opt for neutrals like black, white, or bisque or choose colors that range from pastels to crayon brights. Try either to keep the finishes of your appliances uniform or to go for true contrast. A refrigerator with an exterior that only resembles stainless steel will suffer by comparison to a nearby range in real stainless steel.

Left: This kitchen is well equipped, appliance-wise, for large-scale entertaining. A pair of wall ovens supplements the commercial-style range, making it easy to prepare multiple courses at one time.

Left: A warming drawer can keep foods at their optimum serving temperature. Next to the range is a good spot to install one—or put a unit in an island near the dining area.

Below: New appliances with European styling can be so sleek as to almost disappear. With knobs dropped down to the cabinet front, this electric smoothtop makes its presence obvious only when turned on.

Small appliances, particularly microwave ovens, have jumped in with some big ideas. To speed up everyday tasks, you'll find hot combinations like microwave-toasters that conserve counter space. They function like microwave ovens but also toast, broil, and bake like a toaster oven. Another version brews coffee instead of browning toast. And built-in espresso systems make grabbing a latte as easy as pushing a button.

Manufacturers are continuously rolling out models in every appliance category to complement the latest kitchen trends. You'll see examples on the following pages. To help you zero in on what to buy, see the appliance shopper's guides on pages 94–107.

Right: This European range works differently than its American cousins. It's always on, and the cooking elements and ovens operate at fixed temperatures.

Below: A colorful 1920s yellow-and-green range, discovered at a yard sale, was restored to give character to a remodeled kitchen.

Above: Refrigerator drawers are a handy supplement to a full-size refrigerator, perfect for snacks for kids or the essentials for a well-stocked bar.

Right: Sliding glass "barn" doors shield the laundry area from this kitchen but still let in light.

Stainless-steel appliances have a clean, contemporary look that complements almost any decorating mode, including this modern farmhouse style.

Left: In this well-planned kitchen, the refrigerator and the wall oven can be opened without banging into each other. Be sure your floor plan allows unrestricted access to all your appliances.

Below: A refrigerator this imposing would grab the spotlight without panels that match the adjoining cabinets. Now it blends in nicely with its surroundings.

UNIVERSAL *Design*

Planning a kitchen that offers easy access for people of all abilities and ages is what universal (barrier-free) design is all about. Here's how to bring these design principles home.

Appliances. Select models that are convenient to access while seated, like side-by-side refrigerators and side-hinged ovens. Other functional setups include wall ovens installed low enough to use while sitting down, cooktops with front-mounted controls, and dishwasher and refrigerator drawers, which minimize bending.

Clearance. Leave space below both sink and counters to allow room for a wheelchair or for those who need to sit while they work. (Plan to enclose the plumbing to prevent contact with hot pipes.)

Hardware and controls. Exchange standard doorknobs, faucet handles, and cabinet hardware for levers and pulls that can be operated with one closed hand or wrist. Magnetic touch-and-release closures are ideal for doors.

Maneuverability. To accommodate a wheelchair, the door into the kitchen should be at least 32 inches wide, while traffic aisles should be 42 to 48 inches wide. Plan turnaround space near the sink and major appliances.

User-friendly heights. Counters of more than one height let a seated cook work side by side with one who is standing. Locate frequently used storage between 15 and 48 inches high. Doorknobs and handles should be no more than 48 inches off the floor; light switches and other controls, too, should be placed at a convenient height. Pull-out cutting boards, shelves, and trash bins provide accessible work, storage, and cleanup areas.

Visual comfort. Boost task lighting for older users. Incorporate dark and light work surfaces for better visual contrast with cooking ingredients and tools (dark on light, light on dark). Aim for matte finishes rather than glaring, glossy surfaces.

The kitchen below is designed for accessibility, whether in a wheelchair or not. The spaces beneath the island and counter are mostly unobstructed, while utensils hung low on a rack are easy to reach.

An all-in-one micro-wave, light fixture, and vent mounted above the range is a smart solution for cramped quarters. The cooktop is gray ceramic glass that doubles as counter space when not in use for cooking.

Left: Three ovens (two in the range, one built in) give you more options than the standard single-oven range. However, a large turkey probably won't fit in any of them—something to keep in mind when you select your appliances.

Above: Placing an oven low on the inner side of an island allows for an unbroken line of cabinetry elsewhere. Pedestals support the cast-glass countertop above the oven, creating a unique undercounter display area.

Left: For a range this size, allow plenty of landing area on either side for moving pots on and off the burners and resting casseroles and cookie sheets on their way in or out of the oven.

Above: Open shelving keeps this kitchen looking airy but eliminates the full wall that would be needed for a double oven. With plenty of base cabinets, it wasn't a problem to install two single ovens below the countertop.

Right and above: The two main appliances in this elegant country kitchen are treated quite differently: the refrigerator is disguised by panels in the same cream-colored glaze as the cabinets that surround it. The restaurant-style range, on the other hand, is a standout against a back-splash of decorative tile.

Above and right: This expansive kitchen is well organized for family meals or many guests. Ready for large-scale cooking and storage are the dual-oven commercial range, microwave oven, side-by-side full-size refrigerator-freezer, and warming drawer in the island (right). An extension of the countertop (above right) is a cozy spot to check a recipe, sip a cup of tea, or chat with the cook.

Bright *Ideas*

A KITCHEN REMODEL IS THE PERFECT OPPORTUNITY to transform a dim space into one that's cheery even on the dreariest of days. The right windows will bring in natural light, and a good lighting plan will extend daytime brightness into the evening hours with shadow-free, nonglaring illumination and focused task lighting. A visit to a lighting showroom will spotlight the latest options.

To make the most of both natural and artificial light, opt for glossy surface materials, from polished stone and glazed or glass tile to high-sheen cabinets and stainless-steel appliances. Light-hued wood, pale colors on walls and ceiling, and warm-toned countertops and flooring can also boost the glow.

Natural light

Shape and size are especially important for kitchen windows. For instance, clerestory windows at the upper edge of a wall can visually enlarge a room as they allow light to wash across walls and ceiling. Bay and bow windows also expand space; they're a popular choice for spreading light around breakfast nooks and dining alcoves. Skylights and glass doors are another way to increase light and create a sense of spaciousness.

Kitchen windows that face the street or peer into a neighbor's house raise privacy issues,

Left: Translucent cabinets look luminous and keep the kitchen as open-feeling as possible. The window backsplash lets in more light as well as fresh air.

especially if you prefer not to use window coverings. One solution that's both practical and decorative is to specify windows that combine clear glass with translucent, semi-translucent, or textured glass. A retro option is glass block, a stylish throwback to the 1940s and 50s that's attracting new fans for the way it admits soft, diffused light while also providing privacy, security, and insulation. You'll find glass block in different surface textures and sizes.

Light fixtures

The kitchen's expanding role as the nerve center of the home makes good artificial lighting more important than ever. You'll want strong task lighting directly over activity areas. General illumination need only be bright enough to eliminate shadows and ensure safe movement around the room. With multiple sources and dimmer controls, you can turn the light up full throttle when you are working and then gently subdue it after hours.

Keep ease of access in mind when choosing kitchen fixtures, as they'll need frequent cleaning.

Above right: Generous windows and skylights let sunshine flow into this high-ceilinged kitchen. A series of pendants supplies directed task light for the island.

Right: This great-looking window does more than brighten the room. Its perfect proportions provide a design element, too, since it matches the lower cabinet in width and the upper cabinet in height.

Below: Layers of daylight and artificial light—recessed ceiling fixtures, a hanging fixture, and a wall-washing art spot—enhance this dining niche.

Left: Glass block is a good solution when you want to bring in natural light but don't care for the view outside.

Above: A bank of glass-fronted cabinets becomes a see-through divider between kitchen and breakfast nook. The wide pass-through allows each space to borrow light from the other.

Right: The goal was to make this kitchen brighter and more open. The successful makeover added a skylight, replaced a full wall with a half wall on one side, and topped counters with reflective stainless steel.

Below: Laminated glass in both the fronts and the backs of upper cabinets veils the view of the house next door, while clear glass in the backsplash area captures light from a narrow side yard.

FLUORESCENT
Facts

A fluorescent light source uses a quarter to a third of the energy it takes its incandescent counterpart to produce the same level of illumination. That means that a 26-watt compact fluorescent light (CFL) can replace a 100-watt incandescent bulb, and a 13-watt CFL can replace a 40-watt incandescent. And though they cost more initially, fluorescent bulbs can last 10 times longer and cut operating costs by three-quarters. That's why California's new energy code requires that at least 50 percent of the wattage in new or newly remodeled kitchens be high-efficiency —which largely means using fluorescent lights in permanent light fixtures.

Older fluorescent tubes were criticized for noise, flicker, and poor color rendition. Electronic ballasts and better fixture shielding have remedied the first two problems, and new technology has produced many more options in the color of light emitted by fluorescents: you can match the warmth of incandescent bulbs, the cooler blues of halogens, or the full spectrum of sunlight. (The lower a bulb's rating, as expressed in degrees Kelvin on the color temperature scale, the warmer the light color; warm, familiar incandescents range near 2,900 degrees Kelvin, while cooler quartz halogen is rated slightly higher, and summer sunlight higher still.)

Fluorescents are also available in an increasing variety of shapes to fit more kinds of fixtures. CFLs with screw bases directly replace incandescent bulbs in traditional fixtures, letting homeowners conserve energy and reduce electric bills even without remodeling.

In areas that must comply with a code like California's, hardwired kitchen fixtures—from recessed downlights to pendants to under-cabinet strips—must accept a high-efficiency CFL with a pin base. These pin-style fixtures are rated for a specific size and type of fluorescent bulb; when choosing your fixtures, be sure you know which bulbs they accept.

For an overview of California's Title 24 energy code, visit the California Lighting Technology Center at www.cltc.ucdavis.edu.

High-efficiency, long-lasting fluorescent lighting can help you cut electricity costs and be more eco-friendly in your new or remodeled kitchen. In some energy-conscious regions, fluorescents are required for any new kitchen.

Above: The homeowner's passion for glass is reflected throughout this stunning kitchen—on the backsplash and island counter, in the upper cabinet doors, and along the narrow "sill" shelf. Windows above the sink are sandblasted for privacy.

Left: This 1923 bungalow kitchen is cheerful and charming. To balance the light from the back door and banquette windows, the sink windows were lengthened and the sill was eliminated.

Above left: A pivoting floor-to-ceiling window blurs the line between inside and out; frosted glass for windows that face the neighboring house maximizes daylight while restricting the view from outside. Clear glass is used for higher panes.

Above right: This simple, well-lit glass-tile backsplash is highly reflective. At night, it brightens the busy cleanup area around sink and dishwasher.

Left: The challenge was to brighten this compact kitchen and provide access to the patio. The new Dutch door acts as backdrop for an eating counter, pass-through to the yard, and source of light.

Right: Light pours into this kitchen from a quartet of skylights. Tall walls are made for uplighting: a pair of sconces bounces light off the vaulted ceiling.

Above: At a breakfast bar, cabinets with see-through doors and recessed lights show exactly where to reach for a coffee mug and a plate for your morning toast.

Left: To capture light for a dim kitchen, the solid door to the adjoining laundry room was replaced with a multipane one. The ribbed glass, repeated in the upper cabinet, obscures the view but doesn't block the light.

Elegant *Options*

THE KITCHEN MAY BE THE LAST PLACE you'd expect to find standard living-room features like fireplaces, media centers, and stand-alone furniture, but that's exactly where they're turning up. Sharing the spotlight are such envy-inducing extras as built-in espresso makers, wine coolers, and pizza ovens. As the kitchen morphs into the family hangout, more and more of these stylish details are showing up.

On the following pages you'll see a range of amenities, simple to sumptuous. Some speak directly to the serious cook. Warming drawers and heat lights, for example, hold plates and prepared food at ideal serving temperature. Also tempting are conveniences like undercounter refrigerators and dishwasher drawers. Some innovations have been plucked from restaurant kitchens, like a commercial-style pot filler behind the cooktop or range to reduce trips between sink and stove.

Then there's the "good stuff" for the rest of the family. Maybe they'd like built-in speakers connected to a central home audio system (it's a good idea to have a separate volume control in the kitchen). Or does the family wish list include a large-screen television or full-blown home theater and comfortable seating?

Left: A range hood fitted with radiant heat lamps copies a restaurant trick for keeping food warm. The wire shelf below the lamps is designed to hold plates.

You'll find small fixes that feel big, like playful cabinet hardware or blackboard paint that lets you display everything from grocery lists to soccer schedules. On a grander scale are custom range hoods that convey Old World style, or design details that showcase beautiful craftsmanship—like a striking concrete countertop and drainboard with decorative inlay.

Befitting its new role as a center for gathering and entertaining, the kitchen is now accessorized just like rooms elsewhere in the home. Antiques and collectibles, from heirloom furniture to vintage maps in beautiful frames, add special character.

From the floor up, here are ways to outfit your kitchen with furnishings and accessories that will make the hub of the house work still better for you. Even one or two of these items can transform a utilitarian room into an exciting living space, proving that you don't need a sky's-the-limit budget and endless square footage to give your kitchen a little star power.

Left and below: With multiple appliances, open and closed storage, buffet, and large island, this kitchen can handle a crowd. Metal bars set into the countertop act as a permanent trivet, protecting the wood against burns from hot pots. The wine chiller (at left below) has pull-out shelves for quick identification of any vintage.

Above: Another good idea borrowed from restaurant kitchens: a flexible pull-out faucet (left) that can be operated with one hand, a real convenience. A warming drawer (right) will keep the main course hot throughout the meal, so "seconds" will always taste just made.

Right: A movable spigot installed above the stove—a commercial pot filler—eliminates the need to carry heavy, water-filled pots from sink to stove.

Below: This mixer shelf (left) does the heavy lifting for you, and locks in place for stability. When not in use, it retreats into the cabinet. A multipurpose "cook sink" mounted in an island (right) contains a steamer for cooking vegetables or pasta. Remove the steamer insert and it can be used as a regular sink. A fanciful mix of marble and honed limestone forms the countertop.

Above: A prized French walnut cupboard, built circa 1830, holds pride of place as a kitchen hutch. Its handsome styling and warm tones were copied in the kitchen's built-to-spec island (see photo on page 27).

(see photo on page 27)

Below: What looks like a cabinet is actually an undercounter refrigerator, installed to hold beverages for both entertaining and everyday needs.

Above: Beautiful details convey Old World ambience. The custom range hood is finished with layers of plaster, sealed to preserve the neutral color. Intricate Celtic patterns ornament the tile backsplash.

Left: Dishwasher drawers wash small loads efficiently. With custom fronts, they disappear into cabinetry.

Right: This bank of appliances—a professional-style espresso maker on top and a multirack steamer below—takes you from breakfast to dinner.

Left: Food isn't the only reason to check out this refrigerator. With a door that's a chalkboard, it's also the family message center.

Left: A wood-fired pizza oven delivers the goods to an adjoining built-in booth. The Italian-made oven is based on a dome-shaped terra-cotta insert, surrounded by fireproof tiles, brick, and insulation—all covered in plaster.

Above: Entertainment areas with big-screen televisions, fireplaces, and cushy seating are increasingly popular in large, open-plan kitchen designs, making this room much more than just a spot for cooking and eating.

ANCHOIS
SARDINES AU BARRIL
CONSERVERIE

How to
DO IT

SAVORING A VISION OF YOUR DREAM KITCHEN? Hold that thought. Remodeling involves more than sleek new cabinets and high-tech appliances. First you need a plan that makes every square foot count. Use this section as your remodeling workbook to marry your dreams with practical realities. Which countertop material is best? Do I have room for an island? What type of lighting do I need? We'll help you find the answers that work for you.

Defining
Your Space

BEFORE YOU CAN VISUALIZE your new kitchen, you need a clear picture of the existing space—a floor plan. You may also want to take photographs throughout the project, both to record the before-and-after story and to facilitate repairs down the road: photos showing the location of pipes and wires before they're hidden inside new walls will pinpoint where to look if there's a problem later.

Measuring the space

An accurate rendering of the room on paper—the floor plan—captures your kitchen as it is now. This will be your most useful tool for communicating with an architect, designer, or salesperson. And if you're short on ideas, the process of mapping out the room may offer some inspiration.

Start by making a rough sketch (don't worry about scale), doodling in windows, doors, islands, and other features. Then begin your kitchen survey, armed with either a folding wooden rule (the pro's choice because it stays rigid when extended) or a steel measuring tape. Measure each wall, at counter height, two ways. First measure in sections—for example, from a corner to the edge of a door, then across the door, then from the far edge of the door to a window, and finally across the window to the far corner; total these figures. Next take an overall measurement

Left: A soaring stainless-steel vent hood and gleaming backsplash emphasize this kitchen's high ceiling and sleek style. Wood cabinets and flooring add warmth.

Top right: Wine-colored slate forms an elegant accent wall and backsplash behind the cooktop. Adding to the glow is under-cabinet lighting.

of the same wall, corner to corner. The two figures should match exactly. Measure the floor-to-ceiling height of each wall the same way.

Jot down each measurement on your rough sketch as you work your way around the room. Add measurements for any other permanent element—an island you intend to keep, for instance.

Making a floor plan

Now use the measurements you've recorded on your sketch to draw your kitchen to scale. You'll need a straightedge—ruler, T-square, or triangle—and some standard drafting paper with ¼-inch squares. (Most kitchen designers use a ½-inch scale—¹⁄₂₄ actual size; that's two drafting-paper squares per foot.) Make right angles exact and draw arcs (with a compass, if you have one) to indicate which way doors and any casement windows swing. Or create your floor plan with a computer and a home-design software program.

The sample floor plan shown at right includes symbols for electrical elements—outlets, switches, and fixtures. Indicate these and anything else that might affect your plans, such as plumbing and gas lines.

SAMPLE FLOOR PLAN

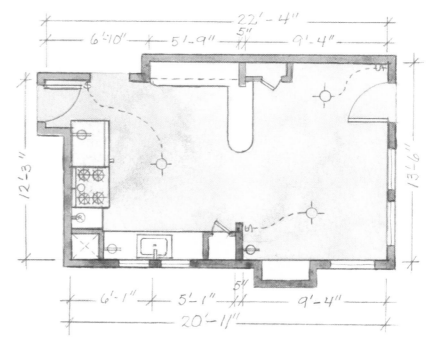

ARCHITECTURAL SYMBOLS

Wall

Window

Door swing

Duplex wall outlet

Wall switch ceiling fixture

Wall fixture

windows

How do you make a kitchen feel bright and airy? The solution usually starts with the style and placement of windows. A well-chosen window brings in the maximum daylight and also connects the cook with the world outside the kitchen.

Below: Walls of windows—awning, double-hung, gliding, and clerestory styles—capture a lake view and lots of natural light in this cheerful contemporary kitchen.

Windows that work

You may be replacing kitchen windows because they are worn out or not energy efficient. Or an altogether new floor plan might require totally new windows. There's an impressive collection of window products to fulfill your needs and bring in daylight where you want it. If you're switching to a different window style or size, check local building codes before buying.

Window options

Window frames come in wood, clad wood, aluminum, vinyl, steel, and fiberglass. Generally, aluminum windows are the least expensive, wood and clad wood the most costly. Vinyl- or aluminum-clad wood windows and all-vinyl windows require little maintenance. What's best for your kitchen depends partly on your home's style and partly on your ventilation needs (for common

types, see "Comparing Window Styles," pages 82–83).

Many of the greatest strides in window technology involve glazing. Ordinary flat glass can now be strengthened, coated, and tinted to block solar heat while letting light in and offering a clear view out. Insulating, energy-efficient glass seals two or more panes together with space between them to trap air. Low-e glass adds a transparent metallic coating that deflects heat—outward in warm weather, inward in cold weather. The coating also blocks the sun's ultraviolet rays, protecting furnishings from fading. Low-e glass is nearly as clear as untreated glass. Some manufacturers use argon gas between panes of low-e glass to further increase energy efficiency.

Overhead styles

Skylights can bring light deep into a room and create a sense of drama where there was merely a blank ceiling before. Early versions earned a reputation for leaks, condensation, or heat loss; but if you buy a quality skylight today and have it installed properly, you shouldn't have these problems.

Fixed skylights vary from square to circular in shape; they may be flat, domed, or pyramidal in profile. Most manufacturers also offer several operable (ventilating) models. A recessed skylight will require a shaft

to direct light into the room below —straight, angled, or splayed.

Roof windows are a cross between regular windows and skylights. Typically installed on sloping walls, these windows have sashes that rotate on pivots on the sides, permitting easy cleaning. ▶▶

Shop Talk

Apron An interior trim piece below the sill.

Casing Wooden window trim, especially interior, added after the window is installed—head casing at the top, side casings flanking the unit. Casings cover the jambs and the gap between the jamb and the rough opening in the wall.

Cladding A protective sheath of aluminum or vinyl covering a window's exterior wood surfaces.

Flashing Thin sheets, usually metal, that protect the wall or roof from leaks near the edges of windows or skylights.

Frame The stationary framework that encloses the sash, consisting of header, side jambs, and sill.

Glazing The window pane—glass, acrylic plastic, or other clear or translucent material. It may be one, two, or even three layers thick.

Grille A removable decorative grating that makes an expanse of glass look as though it is made up of many smaller panes.

Header The top part of a window frame (the bottom is the sill; the sides are the jambs).

Jamb The sides that form a window frame along with the header and the sill. An extension jamb widens a frame to match the window opening in a thick wall.

Lights Separately framed panes of glass in a multipane window, held by muntins.

Low-emissivity (low-e) Describes glass coated with a treatment that sharply improves its thermal performance.

Mullion A vertical dividing piece between windows or between expanses of glass in a single window.

Muntin A slender strip of wood or metal that frames a pane of glass in a multi-pane window.

R-value The measure of a material's ability to insulate; the higher the number, the lower your heating or cooling bills should be.

Sash The framework that surrounds the glass within the window frame; it may be either fixed or operable.

Sill An interior or exterior shelflike trim at the base of a window unit. An interior sill may be called a stool.

U-value The measure of the energy efficiency of all the materials in the window; the lower the U-value, the less energy is wasted.

Comparing Window Styles

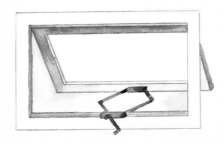

Awning

Wider than they are tall, awning windows are hinged at the top to open outward. Lined up in a row or a column, they are effective both as visual elements and as light producers. They can be installed above a kitchen counter like a back-splash to let in fresh air and light but block most rain.

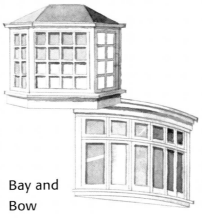

Bay and Bow

A projecting window formed by joining three or more individual windows, a bay often has two smaller operating side windows and a larger fixed center window. A bow window consists of four or more equal-size windows that form a curve. Both types are popular for "stretching" a breakfast area or adding space behind a sink or counter.

Casement

Hinged on the side like a door and opening outward, casement windows are usually taller than wide. They offer unobstructed views and direct fresh air inside. You operate them with a crank—no need to lift or push the window open, a convenience over a sink or an appliance.

Clerestory

Installed near the tops of walls, clerestory windows expand views and let light wash across the ceiling, brightening the room while preserving privacy. These are often small, fixed windows; an operable window installed in this position is either an awning or a hopper.

Double-hung

Sashes that open and close by gliding up or down give these windows a traditional look. They take up no exterior space, making them a good choice where an outward-opening window could be a hazard to those outside.

Fixed

These nonopening windows are used to showcase a view and bring in light (think of picture windows). Often paired with operating side windows, a large fixed window is a good choice in a breakfast area or over a sink. A fixed window may be a significant architectural element—a large triangle set into a peaked ceiling, for instance. Smaller shapes (diamonds, circles) can be interesting accents.

Glass block

A window alternative, glass blocks let in some ambient daylight without sacrificing privacy. They provide even, filtered light that complements many kitchen designs. Many sizes are available; textures include smooth, wavy, rippled, bubbly, or crosshatched. Some are clear, others softly translucent.

Gliding

These easy-to-operate windows have sashes that open like a sliding door—one gliding horizontally past the other. Their clean look suits them perfectly to contemporary homes. Like double-hung windows, they are a good choice where walls abut busy outdoor areas, for the same safety reason.

Hopper

An inverted form of awning window, a hopper is hinged at the bottom and tilts inward. Hoppers are most commonly used in basements but may appear elsewhere, often paired with a fixed upper window.

Below: In this light-filled kitchen, a strip of raised cabinets is supported by the metal frames of a commercial window system. The counter-level windows can open for ventilation.

Document
& Dream

HAVING A CLEAR IDEA about how you want to use your kitchen is as important as choosing what appliances to put in it. To help clarify your needs and wishes, answer the questions on the facing page. Create a planning binder to hold your answers, along with other notes, any clippings you've collected, and a copy of your floor plan (page 79).

What about a Face-lift?

A complete kitchen makeover isn't always possible or necessary, but smaller improvements can have a major impact. Here are some ideas.

- Refacing your cabinets—replacing the existing doors and drawer fronts with new ones—is a speedier, cost-effective alternative to installing new cabinets.

- Consider changing your countertops, especially if they are worn or damaged.

- Give cabinets and walls visual punch with paint. Paint is the easiest, least expensive way to transform a room.

- Change the knobs and pulls on doors and drawers. Just be sure that the new hardware's fasteners fit the old holes.

- Update light fixtures. Some recessed fixtures can accept new trim—a simple change.

- Install new window coverings, or do away with them altogether.

- Cut down on clutter. Make use of the many clever and decorative storage solutions available at home centers and container stores.

Give yourself time

Design professionals advise that you allow at least two or three months for planning, more if possible—even a whole year. Selecting appliances, researching materials, fine-tuning your layout, obtaining permit approvals, and undergoing design reviews—to say nothing of accommodating changes of mind—can each eat up days or even weeks of the project schedule. The tighter your budget, the earlier you need to start planning; tracking down the clever, less costly solutions that are out there takes legwork. Build in enough time so you can make thoughtful choices that mean no regrets later.

Start a wish list. Keep a pad handy by your bed or on a kitchen counter to jot down anything that comes to mind about your current space. List everything you dislike about it and everything you love and might want to replicate. For the moment, forget practicality. Express what you really wish you could have—even if you think you couldn't possibly manage it. A simple or inexpensive solution might present itself later on.

It's not too soon to make decisions about appliances. Do you want a 30-inch range or a 36-inch cooktop with separate 27-inch wall ovens? You can take a new floor plan only so far before you know these specifics.

QUESTIONS
to Ask Yourself

General

- What's your main reason for changing your kitchen?

- How long do you expect to own this home?

- Are you designing the kitchen yourself or working with an architect or designer? Hiring a contractor, acting as your own contractor, or doing the work yourself?

- What is your timetable for completing the project?

- What approvals and/or permits are needed?

- What is your budget?

Scope and function

- Are you considering any structural changes? What's beneath the kitchen—full basement, crawl space, concrete slab? What's above it?

- Can existing doors and windows be moved? Can any interior walls be removed?

- What secondary areas would you like to include in your kitchen—baking center, breakfast nook, media center, laundry center, computer station, wet bar?

- Would you like an island or peninsula? Is there enough space?

- What is your current heating system? Do any walls contain ducting?

- What's the amp rating of your electrical system?

- Can existing plumbing be moved? Where to?

- How many people are in your household? Are any disabled or elderly? How many primary cooks? Right- or left-handed? How tall?

- Which new appliances are you planning to buy? Freestanding or built-in?

- Will you need a ducting vent hood or a down-draft ventilation system?

- What are your storage requirements? Do you like open storage?

- Where will you keep small appliances, like a mixer or a microwave oven?

Design specifics

- What general style would you like for your kitchen (country, for example)? How does that relate to nearby rooms and to your home's exterior?

- What color combinations do you prefer? What appliance finishes do you like?

- What floor and wall treatments do you prefer?

- If you want wood cabinets, what finish do you envision—natural, painted, stained? Light or dark?

- Do you want one material for countertops, or more? Which kinds do you like?

- Do you want a partial or full backsplash? Matching the countertops, or contrasting?

- What kind of light fixtures do you think will work best? What natural light is possible?

Your answers to the questions on this page will form a good starting point for discussing your ideas with designers and showroom personnel. Write them on a separate piece of paper and keep them in your planning notebook, along with images of favorite kitchens and style details collected from magazines and books. Once you've gathered these planning tools, you're ready to move on to "Layout Basics" in the following section.

Layout
Basics

YOU'RE READY TO PLAN a new kitchen that's tailor-made for you and your household. Review your answers to the questionnaire on page 85, filter your wish lists through the realities of the space you have, and get ready to make some basic decisions. Expect to go back and forth, weighing your options, blocking out work centers, double-checking heights and clearances.

Where to start?

With new construction, you have fewer constraints than if you're remodeling. More often, though, an existing setup drives the plan. Layouts flow from structural realities such as where doors and windows need to be, where the existing plumbing runs, and where there's a full-height wall for a refrigerator. Traffic flow in the kitchen and access to other rooms and to the outside are also critical considerations.

To help focus your planning, this section offers basic layouts, ideas for logical task areas, and specifications for functional work surfaces. Develop two or three trial floor plans. You can draw templates of cabinets and appliances to scale or purchase them ready-made at art supply stores or home centers. Or use computer software designed for creating floor plans. An online search will locate helpful interactive guides for kitchen planning

Left: A functional layout minimizes steps for the cook. Here, the sink, the cooktop, and the refrigerator (partly visible at right) form an efficient work triangle.

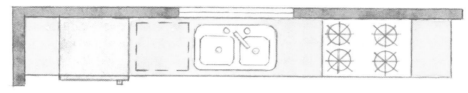

ONE-WALL

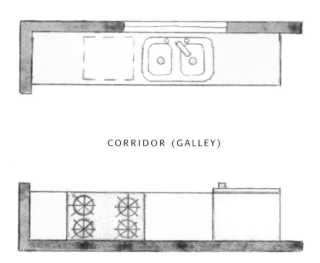

CORRIDOR (GALLEY)

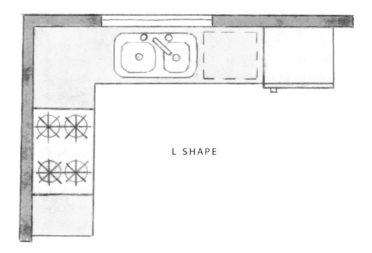

L SHAPE

offered by manufacturers and trade organizations.

Think about the pros and cons of each plan: for instance, one might offer more counter space but less storage. Mentally cook a meal in each layout. Scramble some breakfast eggs and think about every step—get the pan, get the wooden spoon, open the refrigerator, whip up the eggs, cook them, transfer them to a plate, and serve them. Can you do it with ease? The goal here is to reveal flaws—things that won't work for you even though the plan seems perfect on paper.

Common kitchen layouts

Designers say clients rarely ask for a specific kitchen layout, like a galley or U-shaped plan. But it does help to have some basic schemes in mind as you develop your layout. Adapt, combine, or expand these layouts to suit your needs.

One-wall kitchen. Small or open kitchens frequently incorporate a single line of cabinets and appliances. This results in a lot of moving back and forth for the cook—not ideal, but the only option in some cases.

Corridor (galley). This type of kitchen, open at both ends, works well as long as the distance between opposite walls isn't too great. Traffic flow can present a problem—it's tough to divert kitchen cruisers away from the cook.

L shape. A layout utilizing two adjacent walls puts some space between the work centers. Typically the refrigerator is at one end of the L, the sink in the center, and the range or wall oven at the other end.

▶ ▶

U shape. Three adjacent walls make up an efficient U plan that works if there's enough distance between opposite walls. Often this opens up space for additional work areas—a second sink, a baking center, even a complete station for a second cook.

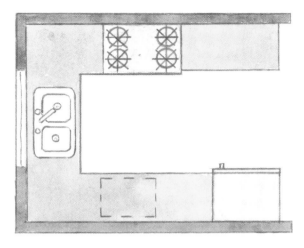

U SHAPE

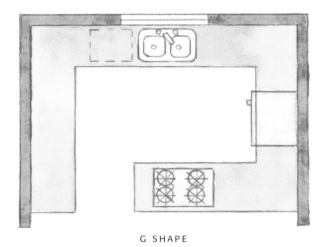

G SHAPE

G shape. Combining the efficient U-shaped layout with a peninsula, the G is a good fit for specialized work centers and helps shield the cook from distracting traffic. However, this arrangement may seem slightly claustrophobic to some cooks.

Islands and peninsulas. A kitchen island can add storage and work space, block unwanted traffic, and provide an eating counter. On the minus side, islands and peninsulas are space hogs, can block the cook's movement, and may impede other kitchen traffic. If yours has a cooktop, you must install a ducted overhead ceiling vent, which can block views, or opt for a downdraft ventilation system that's less intrusive but also less effective. It's usually easier to bring utilities to a peninsula than to an island.

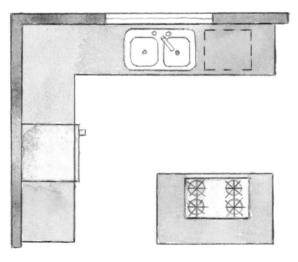

ISLAND

Thinking outside the triangle

Is the reign of the work triangle—imaginary lines connecting the refrigerator, sink, and cooktop—over? Yes and no. Devised in the 1950s, this triangle ensured that a cook need take minimal steps to move among the key work areas, free of obstacles. But the elements of a kitchen layout, and a single cook, are no longer givens. Common today are plans that accommodate dining or family rooms, multiple cooks, islands and peninsulas, entertaining areas, or independent work centers co-opted from restaurant kitchens (see "Working in the Zone," page 90).

After studying many efficient kitchens, big and small, the National Kitchen and Bath Association devised 40 guidelines for planning kitchen layouts. See www.nkba.com for the complete set of guidelines, including the work triangle. Like today's kitchens, they're not one-rule-fits-all. Use them as designers do, as a starting point. Based on these guidelines, here are some considerations to keep in mind when planning your core work areas.

Cooking. Allow a minimum of 15 inches of countertop on one side of the range or cooktop and 12 inches on the other. This creates landing areas for hot pans and allows pot

Above: This wood-framed island serves as breakfast bar, room divider, work area, and gathering spot. The utility sink is handy for prepping vegetables and rinsing hands.

handles to be turned to the side for safety while pots are in use. Follow manufacturer's instructions for clearances if the cooking surface meets a tall end cabinet. Allow at least 9 inches of countertop behind a cooktop for safety in an island or peninsula.

Plan for 15 inches of countertop next to a wall oven or above an undercounter oven. If the oven doesn't open into a major traffic area, the 15 inches can be opposite it—but not more than 48 inches away.

Food prep. You might have more than one of these (see "Working in the Zone," page 90). Locate the primary meal preparation area between a sink and the cooktop or range. Or put it opposite the refrigerator on an island or peninsula supplied with a secondary sink and a cooktop. Plan a minimum of 36 inches of countertop. For adjacent work centers, add 12 inches of countertop. If two cooks work simultaneously, plan at least 36 inches of counter space for each

(a second sink is a boon, too).

Refrigerator. For a grocery landing area, allow at least 15 inches of counter space on the handle side of the refrigerator, or on either side of a side-by-side model or above an under-counter unit. If that's impossible, have the space no more than 48 inches away. The refrigerator door should open away from the core work area. Don't forget to take into consideration the swing radius of refrigerator doors; nothing should block access to shelves and bins.

Sink/cleanup. Since the sink gets more use than anything else in the kitchen, try to place it in the center of the cook's work path. The ideal spot is between the refrigerator and the cooking surface. Allow at least 24 inches of counter space on one side of the primary sink, 18 inches on the other. Clearances for an auxiliary sink elsewhere in the kitchen can be less—3 inches and 18 inches. Include a waste receptacle near each sink, but not necessarily beneath it. Consider a bin for recycling, too, here or nearby.

Locate the dishwasher within 36 inches of the primary sink. Whether it's to the right or left is your call; choose whichever is most comfortable for you.   ►►

WORKING
in the Zone

One key to planning an efficient kitchen layout is to divide the work centers into task zones. Allow for both adequate counter space and storage in each area.

Few cooks actually work alone in the kitchen. Someone may be alongside chopping vegetables, setting the table, or cleaning up. Perhaps there are multiple cooks. Or maybe the kids are doing homework at the kitchen table as dinner prep gets under way. To impose order on potential chaos, restaurant kitchens organize space into separate but interrelated work zones called stations. It's a system of peaceful coexistence that suits today's multi-use residential kitchens so well that it's become a trend.

The core areas of cooking, prep, refrigeration, and cleanup are givens (see "Thinking outside the triangle," page 89). Serious home bakers often add a baking center, complete with a cool marble surface for rolling pastry. Entertaining centers with undercounter wine and beverage refrigerators and storage for barware and snacks are newly popular. They're often removed from the heart of the kitchen to draw guests away from hectic dinner prep.

What zones might work for you? Ask yourself if there's an activity you do so often that a dedicated setup would be really helpful. If the family computer is in the kitchen, zone that space with a desk or work surface, chair, file storage, telephone line, and bookshelves. The point is to cluster related tasks in one area so you can work with as few steps as possible and minimal intrusion from other activities.

Left: You can create a dedicated spot for entertaining in very little space. Tucked into a pantry, this one offers a refrigerator and a wine cooler under the counter, with handy storage above.

Heights and clearances

Standard depths and heights for kitchen cabinets and shelves are shown at right, along with recommended heights for stools, desktops, and dining counters. Counter heights reflect industry standards, but you may wish to customize them to your own requirements (though it's wise to consider how future cooks will view these alterations; keep your home's resale value in mind). The prep center is a good place to customize counter-top heights; guidelines suggest that the ideal height for chopping is 2 to 3 inches below the cook's flexed elbows. Some bakers prefer their work area to be slightly lower, more comfortable for rolling dough; suggested height is 5 inches below the elbows.

Standard minimum clearances in a well-planned kitchen are shown at lower right. These dimensions ensure comfortable work space for a busy cook (or two), enough door clearance for free access to cabinets and appliances, and adequate traffic lanes for diners moving to and from a breakfast area. No entry, cabinet, or appliance doors should swing into each other.

Corners present a special problem when you are planning cabinet runs. Angled cabinets, blind cabinets, and lazy Susans all offer solutions—just make certain there's enough room between adjacent units to let drawers and doors open freely.

STANDARD HEIGHTS

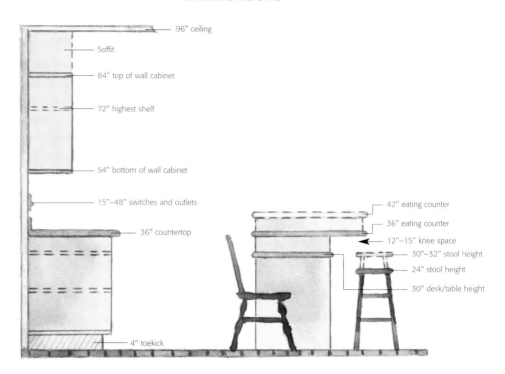

- 96" ceiling
- Soffit
- 84" top of wall cabinet
- 72" highest shelf
- 54" bottom of wall cabinet
- 15"–48" switches and outlets
- 36" countertop
- 4" toekick
- 42" eating counter
- 36" eating counter
- 12"–15" knee space
- 30"–32" stool height
- 24" stool height
- 30" desk/table height

STANDARD CLEARANCES

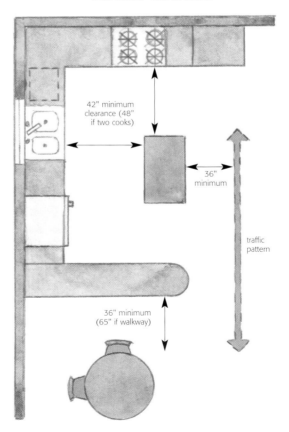

- 42" minimum clearance (48" if two cooks)
- 36" minimum
- traffic pattern
- 36" minimum (65" if walkway)

Appliance *Choices*

DO YOU WANT A TRADITIONAL RANGE, or do you prefer a cooktop and separate wall ovens? Will the refrigerator be built in or freestanding? What type and size of sink seems right? Start research- ing appliances right away—even as you create a floor plan. The ones you choose, and the way you arrange them, will determine the layout for everything else in your kitchen.

Out with the old?

Should you keep your current appliances or replace them? You'll probably be better off discarding any that are more than ten years old, since they're the most likely to break down. Improving energy efficiency is another reason to buy new. It's a more difficult decision with newer appliances. Escalating service calls might push you toward replacement, as might the awareness that sizes can change over time: if your appliances are built in or slide into a run of cabinets, replacements purchased sometime down the road might not fit.

Size, style, cost

New appliances and fixtures could easily add up to tens of thousands of dollars. But choosing the right appliance may not always be a strictly dollars-and-cents decision. For example, finding a wall for the refrigerator could be a challenge in a small kitchen. Is it worth spending more for undercounter

Left: Be sure to include counter space alongside major appliances. You'll need a landing area for hot pans by the stove and one for groceries by the refrigerator.

refrigerator drawers? If you aren't sure, ask yourself if the extra cost is relatively modest in exchange for a more functional layout.

Be knowledgeable about appliance sizes. You'll discover that models of the same nominal dimensions—two 36-inch-wide refrigerators, for example—do not necessarily occupy the same space. A difference as simple as a door profile or a handle projection could cause unexpected fit problems. Factor in design when choosing between seemingly similar types. Can the appliance with a prominent handle open fully without bumping into a cabinet? Will an adjoining cabinet door hit a refrigerator's stylishly bowed front?

Top right: An heirloom range adds vintage character. This one's a standout amid modern cabinets, a high-tech vent hood, and lots of color. **Bottom right:** A single oven installed beneath the countertop is a good solution when wall space is scarce.

refrigerators

Always hardworking, the ordinary refrigerator of past years has now become a kitchen rock star. Popular bells and whistles once found only in high-end units—ice and water dispensers, built-in water filters, stainless-steel finish, glass shelves with spill-trapping edges, adjustable storage, digital controls and displays, and custom decorative panels—have trickled down to mid-level models. And the energy hogs are gone: today's refrigerators are models of energy efficiency.

So many tempting options could lead to impulse choices. You don't want to pay for features that you'll rarely, if ever, use. To shop wisely, it's important to prioritize your needs.

Along with budget considerations, here are some things to think about as you shop for a refrigerator.

Stylish cold storage

Today's trend is toward features that keep your food fresher longer, like multiple storage compartments with separate, adjustable settings for temperature and humidity. Style-wise, cabinet-depth models offer the sleek, integrated look of costlier built-in units. Kitchen decor fully enters into the mix; more style and finish choices than ever before make it possible to match nearby appliances and complement the room as a whole.

Separating top-of-the-line units from the rest of the pack are new configurations that go beyond the standard two-door or door-and-drawer designs. You'll find refrigerators that have four or even six compartments for chilling and freezing, each with its own controls. Interior drawers offer quick-freeze, quick-chill, and quick-thaw options at the push of a button. Some refrigerator doors even come with detachable flat-screen televisions.

For maximum storage, adjacent all-refrigerator and all-freezer models can achieve the look of a single unit by means of a special trim kit. Under-counter refrigerators and freezers, outfitted with doors or installed as self-contained drawers, can function as handy satellites to the main unit. Position them near food prep areas or install them away from where you cook to hold beverages or kids' snacks.

Where do you want the freezer?

Refrigerators come in three basic versions: freezer on top, freezer on bottom, and side-by-side. It's a personal choice, but space limitations might suggest which is best for you.

Top freezer. These offer the most sizes and options for the money. The freezer is space-efficient and conveniently positioned at eye level, but you must bend to access the refrigerator compartment—

Shop Talk

Bottom mount Refrigerator on top, freezer on the bottom.

Built-in Fits flush in a run of cabinets for a sleek, custom look.

Cabinet-depth (counter-depth) A freestanding unit with the almost-flush look of a built-in.

Cubic feet (cu. ft.) Unit of measurement for the usable capacity of a refrigerator and freezer.

Freestanding Any unit that slides into a standard refrigerator opening.

French-door A hybrid style—a split-door refrigerator over a bottom freezer.

Top mount Freezer on top, refrigerator on the bottom.

FRENCH-DOOR REFRIGERATORS

somewhat for shelves, more for low-down crispers.

Bottom freezer. Refrigerated foods, the ones we reach for most often, are at eye level when the freezer is on the bottom. To make frozen items more accessible, manufacturers are fitting freezer drawers with pull-out shelves and tip-out bins. Bottom-freezer units that have split (French) refrigerator doors—requiring minimal swing room—are good choices when space is limited or high style is a goal. Unlike a conventional side-by-side, their full-width shelves accommodate everything from a big turkey to a tray of hors d'oeuvres.

Side-by-side. Vertical compartments put the freezer on the left, the refrigerator on the right. Slender doors have a tight swing radius that is a boon in small spaces. But the narrow compartments make it more difficult to store wide items, and the door swings can block countertop access on both sides. Side-by-sides often cost more than other styles but offer more features. Most have in-door ice and water dispensers—especially popular with families.

Freestanding or built-in?

The other basic decision is whether you want a standard freestanding unit, a built-in, or the recently introduced cabinet-depth option.

What do you have room for? Are you keeping your current cabinetry? A new refrigerator is often deeper than a comparable older model, so a standard unit will stick out more.

Measure the height, width, and depth available for the refrigerator—and be sure you have enough clearance for delivery to the kitchen.

Freestanding. The most common type of refrigerator sticks out about 6 inches beyond the usual 24-inch-deep base cabinets. Visible sides can be finished with optional panels to coordinate with kitchen decor. Choose from bottom-mount, top-mount, or side-by-side units. ▶ ▶

CABINET-DEPTH

Built-in. These high-end units—the most expensive option—give a seamless line to a cabinet run by fitting flush with counters. Most models offer interchangeable panels to match surrounding cabinetry or decor. Top-fitted condensers and compressors add height, which may necessitate custom overhead cabinets. One minus (besides the price) is the relatively shallow interior. Built-ins are available as top or bottom mounts, side-by-sides, or all-refrigerator or all-freezer units.

Cabinet-depth (counter-depth). Unlike the built-ins they emulate, these freestanding units don't require costly custom cabinetry, but they are still higher-priced than regular freestanding refrigerators. They sit almost flush with counters in standard refrigerator openings, freeing up floor space, and they allow overhead cabinets. Many models accept custom panels.

Storage Efficiency

A refrigerator runs best when it isn't stuffed to the gills. As a rule of thumb, you need at least 8 cubic feet of refrigerator space for two people; add 1 cubic foot for each additional person and 2 extra cubic feet if you entertain frequently. Two cubic feet per person is the rule for a freezer compartment.

Choose a refrigerator that's as spacious as you can fit into your kitchen and your budget, with efficient storage that's easy to load and unload. See-through bins and drawers let you view the contents at a glance. Dedicated storage—for soda cans, for instance—is handy if you need it, wasted space if you don't. At the appliance store, mentally stock the model you are considering with the groceries you will store in it. Does it work? If not, keep on looking.

BUILT-IN

SMALL-WORLD
Appliances

Kitchens are expanding in size as they expand in function, and manufacturers are responding by boosting the dimensions of major appliances. As a result, it can be a challenge to find space-friendly units for a kitchen that bucks the trend toward big.

The good news: you do have choices, though they are limited. Compact appliances remain a niche category, geared to satisfy the needs of apartment or condominium dwellers or homeowners outfitting the kitchens of in-law units. You won't see many of them on the floor at appliance showrooms; ask the salesperson what's available to order. An online search may produce the most choices.

You may end up paying more for an appliance with less capacity than for a full-size one. Is your priority more counter or storage space, or is it getting the most from your appliance budget? In very small kitchens, your floor plan may dictate the answer. In any case, consider all your options before you decide how to allot your space and remodeling dollar. Here's what's out there.

Cooktops and ranges. Standard models begin at 30 inches wide, but there are some compact

24-inch gas and electric cooktops and 24-inch-wide ranges. High-end modular cooktop units are 12 to 15 inches wide, offering a choice of gas, electric, or induction heat.

Dishwashers. Standard models are 24 inches wide; dishwasher drawers range from 16 to 24 inches wide. You can find an 18-inch-wide conventional unit. An unconventional option offered by one manufacturer is a double sink that converts to a dishwasher on one side.

Refrigerators. Choices for smaller units are shrinking as conventional refrigerators expand in size to meet federal energy-efficiency standards. The typical unit is now 36 inches wide, but models as small as 18 inches in width are available. Think about capacity: a 24-inch unit typically offers less than 12 cubic feet of cold storage (versus a minimum of 18 cubic feet for a standard refrigerator). Is that enough for your needs?

Wall ovens. Gone are the days when 24-inch-wide units were the norm. The standard now is 27 inches, but a few manufacturers still offer 24-inch ovens.

Installing small-scale appliances is one way to ease the space crunch if your kitchen is short on square footage. Your choices range from basic models to junior versions of professional units.

ranges, cooktops & ovens

PRO-STYLE DUAL-FUEL RANGE

What's better, a separate cooktop and oven (or ovens), or a range that contains both in a single appliance? A wall oven plus a separate cooktop maximizes the flexibility of available space and lets two people work together comfortably—while one cook sautés chicken breasts, the other has room to pop in a sheet of cookies for dessert. And wall ovens are generally positioned at convenient eye level, whereas you've got to bend to use the oven in a range. Still, an imposing pro-style range with six burners can be a glamorous element in a kitchen.

Kitchen hot spots

You can prepare delicious meals with four basic burners and one oven. Serious cooks, though, often seek ranges, cooktops, and ovens that offer greater versatility and convenience. Commercial-style gas burners have heavy cast-iron grates that transfer heat quickly. High-end gas and electric units offer flexibility, cranking out ultra-high heat for rapid boils and quick sears or maintaining a steady whisper of low heat to simmer delicate sauces or melt chocolate.

Glass-ceramic electric units with expandable (dual) elements can effectively heat different pan sizes. Two ovens providing a combination of heating options—conventional heat, convection, steam, microwave—let you cook several courses at once with the method that's right for each.

Think about your personal cooking style, what you have room for and can afford, and the overall look of your kitchen. Then configure your cooking gear to match.

Ranges

If you are remodeling, you have many choices. But if you are purchasing a new range to fit into your current kitchen, size is a factor in what you buy, as are your fuel options. Are you currently set up for gas, is the kitchen all-electric, or can you opt for a dual-fuel range?

A standard unit is 30 inches wide and usually comes with a single oven; if it does have two, neither will be very large (will your Thanksgiving turkey fit?). Pro-style ranges do provide stylish choices in this size category. If you have the space and feel you need two good-size ovens, consider large commercial-style ranges, which are 48 inches wide or more with a pair of ovens.

Most new ranges have self-cleaning ovens and one or more high-power gas burners or expandable (dual) electric elements. Spend more and you'll get more: greater power, more high-heat burners and elements, a convection oven, continuous grates or bridge elements, sealed burners, digital touchpad controls, a warming drawer, and more attention to design.

Finishes match other kitchen appliances, including restaurant-style stainless steel as well as white, black, and bisque. A few high-end models offer color panels or darker metallic skins.

Commercial and pro-style. Professional ranges have been much in demand in recent years—partly due to their higher BTU output and partly because their stainless-steel construction implies serious culinary business. Pro-style (residential/commercial) ranges have the commercial look and the high BTU output of professional ranges and cooktops but with better insulation and such niceties as electronic ignition, sealed burners, heavy continuous grates, and self-cleaning ovens.

MODERN "HEIRLOOM" RANGE

Freestanding, slide-in, drop-in. Freestanding ranges, the least expensive type, can sit anywhere, since

they are finished on the sides as well as the front; controls are on a backsplash. Slide-ins look more custom, with front controls and sides meant to fit between cabinets. Drop-ins rest on a wood platform within base cabinets to blend with the countertop; their integral rims seal any food-collecting gaps.

Heirloom. Popular for period homes, heirloom ranges can be either refurbished oldsters with few modern amenities or high-ticket new ranges with state-of-the-art features and an "old" façade—perhaps in a retro color like mint green or aqua. ▶▶

SMOOTHTOP ELECTRIC RANGE

Shop Talk

BTU (British thermal unit) Measurement of heat output, used for gas burners. One BTU equals the amount of heat needed to raise the temperature of 1 pound of water 1 degree F. The higher the BTU, the more heat a burner produces.

Continuous grates/bridge elements Abutting grates on gas cooktops; elements linked beneath the surface on smoothtops. These features let you move pots smoothly and safely from one burner to another or use cookware that spans two burners.

Convection oven Uses an internal fan to circulate hot air inside the oven, cutting cooking time by a third and lowering required cooking temperatures. Convection heat is tops for roasting and baking; its even air temperature lets you bake food on multiple racks at the same time.

Conventional (radiant-heat) oven The default heat technology for standard ovens, with heat coming from the top and the bottom.

Dual-fuel range Pairs the responsiveness of a gas cooktop with the superior temperature control and better self-cleaning function of an electric oven.

Sealed burners Burners set in depressions that are continuous with the cooktop, so boilovers can't drain beneath the cooking surface.

Speed oven A super-fast oven that cooks with a combination of technologies in a single unit—microwave and convection; microwave and halogen light; or microwave, conventional heat, and convection. (Advantium and Trivection are two manufacturer's model names.)

Cooktops

For flexibility, specialized cooking, or simply a modern look, a separate cooktop makes good sense. Cooktops are also the way to go for kitchen islands and peninsulas—another reason their use is on the rise.

The same considerations apply for a cooktop as for a range. What size? What style? Which fuel? Gas units heat and cool quickly, and the flame is visible and easy to control. Electric units heat faster and maintain low,

even heat better than gas, but you can't adjust the heat as quickly. A few models offer dual fuel, with both gas burners and electric elements.

Mind Your BTUs

Here's how to utilize your gas burners' BTUs for cooking.

■ Simmering—5,000 BTUs (low power/small burner).

■ Everyday cooking—7,000 to 9,000 BTUs (medium power/large burner).

■ Sautéing, stir-frying, searing—12,000 BTUs (higher power/large burner).

■ Rapid boiling (that big pot of water for pasta)—15,000 BTUs (highest power/large burner).

Standard gas and electric cooktops drop into counters like self-rimming sinks, with connections below. Most have four burners; some have five, six, or even more. The majority are 30 or 36 inches wide; all are at least 2 inches shallower than the standard 24-inch cabinet.

Manufacturers are focusing on power and control, introducing higher-output gas burners; faster-heating, megawatt electric elements; and extra-low-heat systems that hold the simmer for sauces or gently melt chocolate. Keep in mind that unless you buy a down-venting model or install a separate downdraft vent, your cooktop will require an overhead vent hood (see pages 136–137). ▶▶

Left: The hefty front knobs of this six-burner cooktop are typical of pro-style units. Black granite tiles set "on point" make a bold backsplash.

Comparing Cooktops

Gas

The choice of most serious cooks, gas burners respond instantly when the flame is adjusted. Most offer a range of BTU outputs for precise cooking; some use dual-flame (stacked) burners for simmer-to-boil flexibility. Easy-to-clean sealed burners, a common feature, contain spills. Sleek gas-on-glass smoothtops are a recent option. Gas cooktops with 15,000 BTUs or higher are considered pro-style.

Glass-ceramic electric (smoothtop)

Smooth, easy-to-clean glass-ceramic surfaces sit flush with counters for a sleek look. When not heating, they can act as added counter space. Radiant (ribbon) heat elements are sealed underneath the surface. Warning indicators on most models stay on until the top is cool, but it's still best to keep young kids away. Look for flexible elements that expand to match various-size pots, bridge elements for large or noncircular cookware, and variable power.

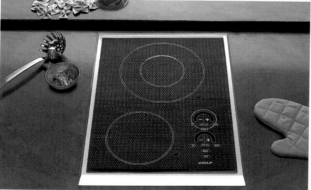

Induction

This is cooking with magnetism, reaching full power in little more than a second. Set a pan in place, turn on the unit, and electricity passes through the glass surface to produce a magnetic field that heats the pan. Remove the pan and there's no live heat source; in effect, the cookware controls the heat. Chefs love induction's ability to slow-simmer. But you must use cookware with magnetic properties—cast iron, porcelain steel, magnetic stainless steel. Induction cooktops are also expensive.

Modular

Individual mix-and-match modules or "hobs," typically 12 or 15 inches wide, offer the ultimate in cooktop customization. These can be grouped together with connecting hardware or embedded in the countertop separately. Among available modules: standard gas, smoothtop electric, barbecue or hibachi grill, griddle, wok, deep fryer, steamer.

Wall ovens

If wall ovens work with your kitchen plan, you'll find the choices in this category far different than in the past. Specialty units designed to complement a conventional oven are one new option. Combinations abound: conventional-convection, convection-microwave, steam-convection, "speed" combinations, and more. More good news: most ovens now have a self-cleaning feature.

If you are replacing a 24-inch-wide wall oven—the most common size in older homes—you'll have limited choices. The typical width sized to fit standard cabinet cavities is now 27 inches; larger ovens are 30 inches or even 36 inches. (If smaller size is a must, consider space-efficient imports from Europe.)

Cooking technologies have impacted oven size, too. In the past, double ovens tended to be two conventional units of the same size. Manufacturers now offer other options, recognizing that most cooks use two standard-size ovens only occasionally. You'll find a full-size oven paired with a smaller secondary oven, taking up less vertical space on your wall than the old setup.

Single ovens. If you have room for only one oven or that's all you need, be sure it's large enough to bake, roast, and broil the foods you prepare most often. Buying multiple single ovens costs more than getting one double unit, but it does let you customize placement, size, and type. Install them below the countertop to open up the wall, either near one another or separated, or side by side in upper cabinetry.

Double/stacked ovens.
True double ovens are connected units, one above the other—a boon for large families and for entertaining. Stacked ovens are individual units installed to present a clean vertical run of appliances. These can be full-size conventional, combination, convection, or microwave ovens. Optional trim kits give smaller-width ovens the built-in look of full-size ones.

Microwave ovens

Foods cook quickly with high-frequency microwaves, but they don't brown. Combination models, like microwave-convection, correct

DOUBLE OVENS

this shortcoming and expand their usefulness; they're increasingly popular as second ovens. (You don't need convection, though, if you only use your microwave to heat coffee or thaw dinner.)

Evaluate the many features available in today's microwaves so that you aren't paying for ones you won't use. All but the cheapest have cooking sensors that shut off power when food is done. Other options include presets for generic food categories (poultry,

MICROWAVE OVEN

frozen entrées, beverages, and so on) plus settings such as add-time, delay start, rapid defrost, and keep warm. Models range from subcompact to family size.

Countertop microwaves can go anywhere, but they take up work space. Built-ins keep countertops uncluttered and have a custom look. Over-the-range models include a vent and cooking lights, but the vents aren't as effective in clearing the air as a regular vent hood. (Some kitchen designers frown on these range-toppers; reaching over burners is a potential hazard, as is having hot food and beverages at eye level or higher.) Brand-new is a microwave drawer designed for islands and under counters; its reach-in access eliminates bending to retrieve dishes or check foods.

High-end microwave ovens offer finishes and exterior styling to match full-size wall ovens; trim kits are optional accessories to give cabinet-installed microwaves a seamless built-in look.

Right: With no room for two full-size double ovens, two smaller appliances (including a food steamer, top) were built in to supplement a generous range (not visible in photo).

Micro Management

If your microwave is built into cabinetry, make sure it's within easy reach for the people who use it most often. Ideally, that's just below the user's shoulder and no more than 54 inches above the floor, according to National Kitchen & Bath Association guidelines.

dishwashers, sinks & faucets

The cleanup center sees lots of active duty in every busy kitchen; in fact, studies show that as much as 50 percent of kitchen time is spent there. It makes good sense to pay special attention to its hardworking components when you're planning your new kitchen.

Waterworks

The traditional single-bowl sink has some serious competition. Today's sink is a multitask center, so double- and even triple-bowl designs are now the norm, equipped with such custom-fitted accessories as cutting boards, colanders, rinsing baskets, and dish racks. Besides these practical innovations, sinks and faucets have also become prime design accents. Faucets are sculptural and decorative, selected as much for looks as for their ability to dispense water.

Dishwashers are becoming quieter as they become harder working. They've even split in half; dishwasher drawers let you wash two loads simultaneously or separately, each at its ideal setting.

Dishwashers

What do we want in a dishwasher? Excellent cleaning ability, whisper-quiet operation, and adjustable racks that accommodate the gamut of cooking equipment and dishes—that's what to look for when you buy a new one.

Shop Talk

Center-set faucets Separate hot- and cold-water controls and a faucet supported on a base or escutcheon, typically found with older sinks.

Farmhouse sink A decorative, old-fashioned sink with a deep, visible front apron, available in a number of materials, colors, and designs.

Integral dishwasher controls Controls inside the door, giving the dishwasher a sleek, uncluttered look.

Single-lever faucets A single fitting that combines the faucet and a lever or knob controlling water flow and temperature.

Spread-fit faucets Separate hot- and cold-water controls and faucet independently mounted on the sink itself or on the deck of the countertop behind the sink.

Left: The brushed finish of the faucet set—soap dispenser, spread-fit "bridge" faucets, and pull-out sprayer—contrasts nicely with this glossy farmhouse sink.

Standard finishes include enameled steel (usually white, black, or bisque), stainless steel, and black glass. Replaceable panels that match base cabinet runs are an option, as are color panels (a current trend) in rich shades like blue, yellow, green, and red.

Sensors and cycles. Most models have soil, temperature, and water sensors—the dishwasher's "brain." These sensors gauge the amount and type of food soil, the size of the load, and the cleanliness and temperature of the water, then adjust performance accordingly. (Prerinsing dirty dinnerware is no longer a must with most current models.) Cycle options include normal, light, pots and pans, quick, rinse/hold, delayed start, "zone" cleaning (top or bottom-rack only), air dry, and delicate (china and crystal). High-end models offer the most cycle choices, but accept that you might pay for settings that aren't useful to you.

Size. Most dishwashers are a standard size: roughly 24 inches wide, 24 inches deep, and 34 inches high. A few compact units and European imports come as narrow as 18 inches. At least one model is an extra-wide 30 inches.

DISHWASHER DRAWERS

INTEGRAL DISHWASHER CONTROLS

Dishwasher drawers, a new concept, divide the standard dishwasher dimensions in half without losing interior capacity. These are good for households that produce repeated small waves of dirty dishes. Stack them or divide them: one on either side of the sink, or one at the sink, another in an island. With custom panels, they practically disappear into cabinetry. One disadvantage: they can't hold extra-tall items.

Sound. Dishwashers were once the noisiest appliance in the kitchen. Improved insulation has hushed their operating levels—in fact, some high-end models are so quiet you might question whether they are even running (a good problem). Manufacturers of ultra-quiet machines

have added lights to tell you whether the load is done or still going, so you don't open the door too soon and get a dose of steam or a spray of water.

Other features. Racks adjust in more ways than ever before—up, down, and even out. Some remove completely to accommodate tall cookware or vent filters. Tines fold flat if you need more room; clips and slots hold stemware. Racks made of coated nylon last the longest. Some models have removable caddies for cooking utensils, tall items, or overflow flatware.

High-end models have a tough stainless-steel tub that attracts heat for efficient drying and won't stain like a white plastic interior—the less-costly but still quite durable alternative. European-made dishwashers use straining filters that you must remove to empty; most others have self-cleaning filters (like small disposers), perhaps more convenient but also noisier.

Many local codes require you to install an air gap unit by the sink along with the dishwasher; this device keeps waste water from backing up if there's a drop in water-supply pressure.   ►►

Left: This seamless stainless-steel sink has a single large bowl and an apron edge.

Sinks

Common sink materials include stainless steel, fireclay and vitreous china, solid surface, enameled cast iron, and composite. More unusual are sinks made of old-fashioned soapstone and concrete. Color-consistent fireclay is gaining in popularity for its high-gloss finish, an alternative to enameled cast iron. For smaller auxiliary sinks in islands or entertaining areas, the burnished glow of copper adds a luxurious note.

If you don't plan to change your countertop, your new sink must fit into the cutout area of the one it replaces. A new countertop frees you to modify your sink's style, size, and configuration.

Sinks are becoming wider and deeper; deeper sinks hold more, but you must bend farther to reach the bottom. Shapes range from geometric squares and skinny rectangles to organic curves. These are style decisions. More practically, calculate the overall counter space available for a sink, then decide how to divide it up. How you actually use your sink will help you pick a configuration.

Single bowl. In small kitchens, a single bowl may be all you have

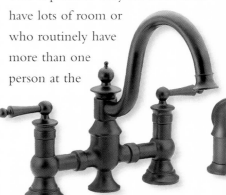

SINGLE-LEVER FAUCET

room for. But even cooks who have a spacious counter may prefer the simplicity of a 30-inch one-bowl sink, especially for washing big items like pasta pots, serving bowls, and baking sheets. And today's high-tech dishwashers cut down on the need to prerinse dishes, which is how a second bowl often gets used.

Double bowl. Scrape and prep in one, wash in another. You can have an even split, with identical bowls; bowls of the same size but different depths; or one bowl larger and deeper than the other. A two-thirds/one-third split works well if both bowls are sizable, but be sure the smaller bowl is big enough to do the job; many are not. Some new styles have a low divider that lets you fill the whole sink for washing bulky items. Where to put the garbage disposer? Wherever you make the mess (see page 116).

Triple bowl. Two bowls of generous size flank a small, shallow prep sink. This is practical only for those who have lots of room or who routinely have more than one person at the

---

Heavy Metal

Popular for their clean, industrial look, stainless-steel sinks suit contemporary and traditional kitchens alike. You'll find them with single, double, and triple bowls; integral drain boards are also available.

The lower the gauge of the steel, the better its quality (18 gauge is best; 22 gauge is flimsy). Composition matters, too. Chrome/nickel blends are the only true "stainless" sinks; cheaper grades will stain. High-quality sinks—those with an 18% chrome/8% nickel content—are stain and corrosion resistant. A matte finish is easiest to maintain and masks scratches better than a mirror finish. Select a stainless-steel sink with sound insulation to mute noise from in-sink disposers or dropped flatware.

BRIDGE-STYLE SPREAD-FIT FAUCET

Comparing Sink Styles

Integral

An integral sink, molded of the same material as the countertop and fused to it, gives a sleek, sculpted look. Materials include stainless steel, solid-surface composite, and concrete; the color can match or complement the countertop. Embellishments include edge banding and other options such as decorative grooving and adjacent drain boards.

Self-rimming/overmount

The least expensive option, drop-in self-rimming sinks are supported by the edge of the countertop cutout. They work well with any countertop material and are a must with tile. Predrilled holes accommodate faucets, air gaps, and accessories like soap pumps; be sure the model you choose works with the items you want, where you want them.

Undermount

Attaching the sink below the countertop gives a clean look that works well with any slab or one-piece installation—natural stone, solid surface, engineered stone, Richlite, stainless steel, concrete, wood. Cleanup is easy—just sweep debris right into the sink (no rims to catch crumbs). Faucets and accessories are installed on the flat deck of the countertop, not the sink itself.

sink at a time; the entire configuration can stretch to 50 inches wide.

Faucets

Popular finishes include polished chrome, stainless steel, nickel, colored enameled epoxy, pewter, polished and antiqued brass, and oil-rubbed bronze. For sheer durability, a faucet that has a high nickel content and softly brushed satin surface is still the best bet. Whatever the style and finish, professionals agree that you get what you pay for. Pricey solid-brass workings and ceramic-disk valve designs repay their cost with greater durability.

Today's kitchen faucets fall into two camps: European-style with pullout sprayers and interchangeable attachments, and traditional projecting or gooseneck faucets with individual handles. (If you need a separate sprayer, buy one made to partner with your faucet.) Regardless of style, the stream from the faucet should start up high enough to fit over a large pan. Water controls must do more than look good;

they must be easy to grip and operate, even when you have wet or greasy hands.

PULL-OUT SPRAYER

If your sink is self-rimming, be sure its installation holes will accept the type of faucet you plan to buy as well as any additional accessories, such as hot/cold water dispenser, soap dispenser, water purifier, and a dishwasher's air gap.

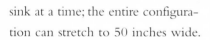

SPREAD-FIT FAUCET

Storage
for Everything

AFTER YOU HAVE SELECTED your appliances and decided where they will go, it's time to plan your storage spaces. Where will you put cookware, small appliances, tableware, and pantry items? You'll want a place for cutting boards, favorite bakeware, everyday paper goods, even the telephone book. A sense of how all of it will be organized will clarify your cabinet requirements.

Left: Traditional closed cabinets aren't the only storage option. Here, open shelving made of metal rods keeps pans within easy reach below the cooktop.

Assigning spaces

Don't wait until you move into your new kitchen to figure out where you want things to go. Faced with the task of emptying dozens of boxes, you might fill drawers and cabinets haphazardly in a rush to restore order. And there it will all stay.

Instead, map out storage that's logical for you. Start by listing everything you plan to store. Open every cabinet and drawer in your existing kitchen and decide for the contents: Do I want to keep it? Where will it go in the new space? Would it be better somewhere other than the kitchen? (Bulk supplies, pet food, even light bulbs might move to a near-by pantry, the laundry room, or the garage.)

Think about specific tasks. As you unload the dishwasher, where will things go? How many steps will it take to put away clean dishes and flatware? Perhaps those items should be stored nearby for convenience. Where is your prep

tea pots
coffee + tea
salad bowls
oils + vinegars
telephone book, pad, pen
plastic wrap, foil, storage bags, napkins
small storage containers
oven mitts, potholders, aprons
SLIDE out double trash cans
dish soap, sponges
dish towels
bowls
vertical storage for trays, cutting boards
plates
flatware
glasses + mugs
casseroles + baking dishes

area? Put cutting boards there. Would it ease the morning rush to group breakfast supplies—cereal, bowls, juice glasses, a toaster or toaster oven—in one storage center? Would it help to have a dedicated coffee bar, with room for a coffee maker, mugs, spoons, and filters?

Measure and mark it down

Use your floor plans to draw elevations. Like snapshots of a finished room, elevation drawings (like the one above) show complete walls with appliances and cabinets in place. Draw them to scale by hand or create them quickly and easily on a computer with a home-design software program.

On your elevations, sketch in potential cabinets and drawers and then designate what will go in each one. Measure the things to be stored: you don't want to discover later that objects you use all the time are too big to put away where they're supposed to go. The goal is to assign an appropriate space to each important thing. Good planning at this stage will help you utilize the space in the best possible way.

You'll find your careful measurements especially helpful when you plan your cabinets. They'll help you decide how to configure a cabinet run—how many drawers and shelves you need, how tall or wide they should be, and how they should be spaced.

Above: Making efficient use of corners is always a challenge. Behind standard drawer fronts, this clever solution allows access to otherwise lost space.

cabinets

Nothing transforms a kitchen more than new cabinets. They establish the room's style and personality and form the backbone of its organization. And nothing that you purchase for your kitchen will cost you more. For all these reasons, it is important that you carefully study the many available options before you decide on this key element.

Closeup on cabinets

Visit a cabinet showroom these days and you might think you're in a

BIRCH; COUNTRY FRENCH

furniture store instead. You'll see furniture-like storage hutches and islands that have feet rather than baseboards, plus architectural details like corbels (brackets used to support shelving) and intricately carved molding. You'll find ultra-modern slab-front styles in beautiful woods and finishes ranging from warm honey or rich chocolate to glossy, bright colors. Then there are two-color treat-ments, with upper cabinets in one hue and base cabinets in another; doors with decorative glass or metal

LAMINATE; SLAB

panels; and a choice of environmen-tally friendly materials for cabinet construction.

Making cabinets easier to use are items such as mechanisms to slow

STAINED PINE; SHAKER

drawers down and keep them from slamming shut. Clever storage solutions give purpose to otherwise dead areas like corners.

All sorts of accessories organize cabinet interiors, from flatware caddies to plate partitions to recy-cling centers.

Decorative hardware comes in an almost endless array. Knobs in faceted glass or stainless steel look discreet, while pulls in industrial-style materials or deep-hued traditional finishes are standouts. Be sure to check whether the hardware is included when you buy your cabinets. If not, that's an extra line item in your budget—but it means you can choose exactly what you want.

Faceframe or frameless?

Selecting doors with arched panels that suggest the French countryside is a style decision. But before you make that kind of choice, you must decide how your cabinet box will be constructed and how doors and drawers will fit into it. You have two basic choices of cabinetry construction, faceframe and frameless (Euro-style).

In traditional *faceframe cabinets,* the raw front box edges are masked by a wood frame. Doors and drawers fit flush in the opening (inset) or cover part of the frame (partial overlay). Because the frame reduces the size of the opening, drawers are narrower than the full width of the cabinet, decreasing their capacity. Door hinges may be exposed or hidden.

The European invention of *frameless cabinets* eliminates the frame altogether. Open the door of a Euro-style cabinet and you see the edges of the box itself; close the door and the edges are covered. Hinges are always hidden.

Shop Talk

Base cabinets/upper (wall) cabinets The cabinets installed below (base) or above (upper or wall) your countertop.

Cabinet box The basic cabinet housing, consisting of a top, a bottom, two sides, and a back; the front is open. Doors and drawers are not included.

Frame-and-panel door A flat, recessed, or raised panel within a frame of two horizontal "rails" and two vertical "stiles." Recessed panels typify Shaker, Arts and Crafts, and transitional styles, while raised panels are common for both traditional and country styles.

Full-extension guides Sturdy hardware that allows drawers to be opened to their full extent, affording a corner-to-corner view of the contents—a sign of quality construction.

Glaze Applied as a finishing treatment over a base color to enhance door and drawer detail and improve or even out the color and appearance of wood.

Slab door A sleek door with no recessed or raised detail, seen most frequently in contemporary settings. Slab drawers also can be used to give a fresh look to frame-and-panel doors and are often used with them in traditional kitchens.

Toe kick A supporting pedestal for a base cabinet, recessed slightly to make room for your toes when you stand close to the cabinet. Toe kicks are attached to traditional cabinets, usually separate with European-style frameless cabinets. A separate toe kick lets you adjust counter height to your liking or stack base units.

Interior compartments like drawers can be sized to practically the full dimension of the box, maximizing storage potential.

These two construction styles determine what choices you have in the way the doors and drawers fit into the cabinet box.

Flush-inset. Only custom cabinetry typically offers this high-end fit, in which doors and drawers close flush with the frame of faceframe cabinets like fine furniture. The most traditional style of cabinet, it's also the most expensive—such a precise fit requires a high level of craftsmanship and takes lots of time to produce. ▶▶

FLUSH-INSET

PARTIAL-OVERLAY

FULL-OVERLAY

Partial-overlay. Part of the face-frame is covered by a lip on the door and drawer edges. Usually traditional in style, these are less expensive than flush-inset doors and drawers because of the slightly forgiving fit.

Full-overlay. Doors and drawers fit to within $\frac{1}{8}$ inch of each other, forming a smooth run that completely covers the boxes of frameless (Euro-style) cabinets with just a sliver of space between them to allow smooth operation. The common choice for contemporary cabinets, full-overlay doors can look traditional when molding is added.

Stock, semi-custom, or custom?

Cabinets are manufactured and sold in three ways: stock, semi-custom, and custom. The type you choose will affect the cost, overall appearance, and workability of your kitchen. But the lines are blurring. Many basic and mid-level cabinets now offer options and accessories formerly considered custom-only, like better drawer guides, pull-out shelves, or fancy molding.

Stock cabinets. The least expensive type, these are mass-produced in limited, standard-size increments. You'll have the fewest choices in box size, door style, and materials. If the dimensions of your floor plan don't match the available increments, you'll have to add fillers that decrease the storage space of your cabinets. Stock RTA (ready-to-assemble) units cost less but require some basic tools and elbow grease for assembly.

Semi-custom cabinets. Perhaps the best option if the price fits your budget, semi-custom cabinets bridge the gap between basic stock pieces and the anyway-you-want-them world of high-ticket custom cabinets. While they are manufactured, semi-custom units are of a higher grade and offer more design flexibility and sizes than stock cabinets—for more money, of course. You can change virtually everything on the basic modules: replace doors with drawers, set a decorative vent hood over the cooktop, add pull-out pantries. Heights, widths, and depths can be modified to fit any design.

Custom cabinets. Unlike off-the-shelf stock cabinets, custom units are strictly made to order, according to a designer or cabinetmaker's exact specifications. Custom cabinet shops

Right: Store-bought stock cabinetry like this system is a money saver, allowing you to customize in other areas.

Below: The casual look of this kitchen results from the mix of dark and light cabinets, while seeded-glass door fronts and open shelving give it a spacious feeling.

can match anything, size truly odd-ball configurations, and create kitchen woodwork that looks like fine furniture. You can't help but notice the difference—joints are seamless, wood is free of any blemish, finishes are as beautiful as on a treasured heirloom. Less eye-catching, but still a hallmark, is the use of superior materials for construction and operation, making custom cabinets both long-lasting and a pleasure to use. Of course, this is the most expensive option.

Hardware details

Doors must open, drawers glide out. To get inside your cabinets without a struggle, you need hardware, a small finishing detail that has big impact in a kitchen. Happily, the selection today is huge, offering choices for every decorating style. You'll find sleek stainless-steel bars, faceted pulls in old-fashioned milk glass, even knobs shaped like moose heads, starfish, or twigs. Or you can opt for a non-hardware look: magnetic touch-and-release closures give you a clean cabinet façade. Sources abound, from traditional hardware stores to designer showrooms to Web sites.

Top: This handsome custom cabinet serves multiple functions: in addition to providing storage and a work surface, it defines the kitchen, dining area, and hall.

Bottom: All the cabinet hardware in a kitchen needn't match. A bronze stick-figure pull adds a touch of whimsy.

Looks count, but well-designed cabinet hardware should be more than just eye-catching. Do you want all knobs, all handles, or a combination of the two? It's more than an aesthetic decision. You want hardware that feels comfortable and affords a good grip. Is the handle deep enough so you can easily slip your fingers around it, or do your knuckles bump against the cabinet?

Try it out yourself, if possible, before making a final decision.

Getting help

Nailing down the style and configuration of cabinets can be easier with professional assistance. Some showrooms, home centers, and big-box stores have full-service designers to walk you through the process, applying any charge against the purchase price of the cabinets. (Be aware that an in-store designer might represent a particular line or just that retailer's products; for a complete overview of what's available, shop around.)

DECORATIVE
HARDWARE

Judging Quality

Why do some cabinets cost more? Here are spot checks to help you determine quality.

Drawers. Think about how many times a day you open and close a kitchen drawer. It's no wonder that good ones make all the difference. You'll pay a premium for such details as solid-wood drawer boxes, dovetail joints, or full-extension ball-bearing guides.

Drawer options include **(top left)** budget-oriented drawer boxes with self-closing epoxy guides; **(top right)** molded metal sides with integral runners; **(bottom left)** sturdy, full-extension, ball-bearing guides; and **(bottom right)** premium hardwood boxes with dovetail joints and invisible, under-mounted guides.

Hinges. Do visible hinges seem sturdy? If hinges are concealed, check for adjustability. Invisible Euro-style hinges can be reset and fine-tuned with the cabinets in place.

Box material. High-end cabinets use plywood rather than particleboard: $1/2$ to $3/4$ inch thick for side and rear panels, $3/4$ inch thick for shelves.

Details. Hardware is distinctive in both design and finish on top-quality cabinetry. Knobs and pulls are comfortable to grip and enhance the cabinet's overall appearance.

trash talk

You'll want to organize your kitchen trash system for efficiency and convenience. Appliance options include an in-sink garbage disposer and a trash compactor. In addition, you'll need a place to temporarily store compostables and recyclables.

Shop Talk

Batch-feed garbage disposer Kicks into gear when you engage the lid; won't start unless the cover is in place. The twist-start lid lets water pass through when the disposer is running, but not solids (or your hand).

Continuous-feed garbage disposer Activated with a wall switch or a sink-mounted, push-button air switch; lets you feed in new scraps as old waste is being ground up and washed away.

Waste not

Most important: decide what type of trash/recycle system your kitchen has room for. Then consider how often you need or want to shift

Below: Sliding drawers for recycling bins, with display space above them, offer both convenience and good looks.

material to a collection point else-where, be it the garage or a shed or curbside bins. Finally, know what local regulations allow or require you to do.

Garbage disposers

A garbage disposer is at the top of the list for most cooks. A disposer will grind almost all types of food waste—chicken bones to citrus rinds—into tiny particles to be swept by running water into your sewage system or septic tank. It keeps food waste from piling up as you work, lessens the volume of trash you must deal with daily, and rids the kitchen of scraps that can attract bugs.

Proponents point out that as disposers drain into waste-water treatment systems, they reduce the amount of solid waste in landfills. But some cities restrict their use, while others require them. Check local codes where you live, and be sure your sewer system or septic tank can support a disposer.

Should you buy a batch-feed or a continuous-feed model? The former

Above: A rectangular metal cover hides a compost bin for produce scraps. The bin sits in a cabinet drawer designed just for it.

is considered safer, especially with kids, but less convenient, since you can grind only one batch at a time. The latter is easier to use and it handles waste more quickly (you don't need to stop to reload), but hands must stay clear of the open filler neck during operation to assure safety.

The best performers have sturdy motors (¾ horsepower or more) that can quickly grind bones to a fine powder; noise insulation; and efficient anti-jam systems.

Trash compactors

Compactors reduce bulky trash to a quarter of its original size, or even smaller. A typical compactor can hold a week's worth of trash generated by a family of four. Be aware that a compactor is for dry, clean trash only—you'll still need other outlets for food waste.

These units are less popular now than they were 20 years ago, probably because more households recycle their trash. Also, opponents argue that compressed trash takes longer to break down in landfills. But homeowners who do have compactors appreciate the way they reduce the volume of trash.

If you're considering buying a trash compactor, look for these features: separate top-bin door for loading small items (even while the unit is operating), activated charcoal filters to control odor, toe-operated door latch, anti-jam system, quiet operation, and key-operated safety switch. Make sure the unit is easy to empty and clean.

Recycling storage

For recycling, opt for convenience. If you have the space, plan for recycling storage units in your kitchen base cabinets. Some sit behind standard cabinet doors, usually as two, three, or four-bin pull-out units. You can also buy special-use base cabinets that have built-in dividers and tilt-down bins. Some rotate in corner cabinets; others glide in and out like drawers. You'll find them at home improvement centers, through catalogs, and as accessories from cabinet manufacturers.

In communities that provide bins, consider pull-out drawers sized to fit them—all you do is remove the bins on pickup day and set them curbside. These require custom cabinets, however.

Try to position recycling containers near where waste is generated. If you have room in the kitchen for only a few small bins, set up a larger bin elsewhere—preferably near where recyclables are hauled away.

Trash bins

You can't compact, grind up, or recycle everything. Every kitchen also needs a basic trash can. Install it behind a cabinet door adjacent to the sink rather than below it, and one person will be able to dispose of table scraps while someone else loads the dishwasher. Locate another near the prep sink, if you have one.

BULLET-STYLE TRASH CAN

Disposer Use and Care

Follow these guidelines to get the best service from your garbage disposer. Run cold water during grinding and for 15 to 20 seconds after to move food along. Feed in vegetable peels gradually. Grind lemon peel to help eliminate odors. Use hard materials like ice and eggshells as "cleansers" to scour the drain chamber. Avoid disposal of grease, which can solidify and clog plumbing. Toss fibrous foods like artichokes and celery stalks in a trash can, along with papery onion skins—they can block the drain.

Texture, Pattern, *and Color*

AN INVITING KITCHEN COMBINES function with good looks. Once you've decided on your basic floor plan, focus on the design details. The materials you choose—their textures, patterns, and colors—will set the room's style and define the space within it. Start by thinking about the following design concepts. Then review examples of decorating motifs beginning on page 24.

Texture and pattern

A kitchen's surface materials may include many different textures—from a smooth tile countertop to an irregularly tumbled stone backsplash, from a pebbly vinyl floor to a tightly woven fabric valence. In general, rough textures tend to absorb light, make colors look more subdued, and lend a feeling of informality. Smooth textures reflect light and often suggest elegance or modernity. Using similar textures helps unify a design and create a sustained mood.

Pattern, too, is an important contributor to a room's style. You'll want your choices to harmonize with the overall feeling of the room. And although we usually associate pattern with wall or window coverings, keep in mind that even wood, stone, and glass create patterns.

Left: In this stylish, casual, and contemporary kitchen, an earthy palette of materials, colors, and textures establishes a feeling of warmth and casual sophistication.

While varying texture and pattern adds interest, too much variety can be overstimulating. It's usually best to let a strong feature or dominating pattern be the focus of your design and choose other surfaces to complement rather than compete with it.

All about color

Use color to highlight your kitchen's architectural features, visually enlarge a small space, or brighten one that's short on natural light. But how do you make sense of the daunting array of paint chips at your home center? The key to a successful color scheme is the color wheel.

The color wheel shows harmonious color relationships and gives helpful color cues. But the appealingly complex colors used by interior designers are rarely the pure orange, red, and violet of the typical color wheel. Instead, they are low-intensity versions of these hues, as shown at right. A quick review of color terminology will let you

browse unfazed through rows of hues, tints, and shades until you find the right palette for your project.

Analogous color scheme. Made up of colors that are side by side on the color wheel: red, red-orange, and orange, for instance. Avoid monotony by using these colors in varied amounts, with one of them as an intense accent.

Complementary color scheme. Composed of colors directly opposite each other on the color ring, like red and green (or approximately opposite—like sage green and violet). Some complements, like orange and blue, can be harsh. But blue and yellow, a combination seen in the garden, is pleasing.

Complex color scheme. Created from colors that are equidistant from one another around the ring. Complex schemes are pleasing because they automatically balance visual temperature.

Monochromatic color scheme. Combinations of different shades of a single color. The effect tends to be restful.

Hue. Just another word for color.

Turquoise and rose are hues, as are lilac and indigo.

Intensity. Is the color bright or dull? Cobalt blue, lemon yellow, and lacquer red are examples of intense blue, yellow, and red. Navy, gold, and cranberry are low-intensity versions of the same colors.

Neutral. Black, gray, and white, sometimes called "non-colors." These true neutrals provide visual relief in a color scheme without altering color relationships.

New neutrals. Very low-intensity versions of colors, or true neutrals altered with a hint of color.

Shade. A color mixed with black.

Temperature. A color's "warm" or "cool" effect. Yellows, oranges, and reds seem warm and cozy. Greens, blues, and violets are cool and serene. But visual temperature is relative: next to orange, red-violet looks cool; next to blue, it looks warm. Balance a cool scheme with a little warmth, and a hot scheme with something cool. Depending on your kitchen's orientation, you could use warm or cool colors to balance the quality of natural light.

Tint. A color mixed with white.

Value. A color's lightness or darkness. Mint is a light value of green. Navy is a dark value of blue.

MEDIUM-VALUE, LOW-INTENSITY COLORS

DARK-VALUE, LOW-INTENSITY COLORS

countertops

hop on it, knead on it, serve from it—you ask a lot, every day, of your kitchen counter-top. One all-purpose surface may have been enough in the home you grew up in. But today's kitchen, as a center of family activity, is increasingly multi-purpose. No one countertop material is perfect for every kitchen task.

ENGINEERED STONE COUNTERTOP

Counter intelligence

The principal countertop materials currently in favor for kitchens are plastic laminate, tile, solid surface, wood, and natural stone—including granite, marble, limestone, and slate. Also showing up on kitchen counters are soapstone and concrete,

along with manufactured materials such as quartz-based surfaces and woodlike compressed composites. Stainless steel, too, draws fans for its contemporary, commercial-kitchen ambience.

You probably already know how many materials look, and you may have a preference based on that. But learn their characteristics (including maintenance requirements) before you make a commitment. Consider where you'll put the material and what tasks you'll use it for. Keep cabinetry in mind, too: you want counters and cabinets to look good together. Use the chart on pages 122–123 to educate yourself about the options.

Consider a mix of materials to put the right work surface just where you need it— resilient butcher block in an island prep area, for instance, with cool marble at a baking center and perhaps heat-resistant natural stone or ceramic tile next to the stove. If you prefer a single

material all around, increase its versatility and prolong its life and its good looks by using tools like cutting and pastry boards, heatproof trivets, and dish racks.

Backsplashes

Today's backsplash—that vertical extension of the countertop just beyond and above the work sur-face—is both a practical kitchen aid and a visual focal point. Its main purpose is to keep the wall clean and stop liquids and food from slipping behind the counter. However, an eye-catching backsplash can play a big decorative role, too.

Here are some ideas to consider when planning a backsplash:

QUILTED STAINLESS-STEEL BACKSPLASH

Shop Talk

Engineered stone The newest category of surfacing material, a natural product most commonly made of up to 95% quartz crystals and referred to as "quartz."

Honed A low-sheen surface with a smooth, matte finish.

Installed price Total cost of materials, fabrication, and installation, usually expressed per square foot.

Plastic laminate The most common countertop, made by sandwiching paper layers between clear plastic that is then bonded to a plywood or fiberboard substrate. The top layer of paper supplies the visible color and pattern. Readymade molded versions are called "postformed."

Polished A sleek, mirrorlike surface that is light reflective.

Richlite The brand name of a tough, paper-based material that has moved from commercial kitchens to homes.

Solid surface A manufactured product that emulates stone (Corian and Wilsonart are two brands), created by combining natural minerals with resin and additives.

Tumbled A surface finish produced by tumbling stone in sand, pebbles, or steel bearings to round off corners and create a rustic, matte finish.

LAMINATE COUNTERTOP WITH METAL EDGING

- Create a composed look by using the same material as for your countertop, perhaps mixing forms—slab on the counter, tiles set on point on the wall.

- For visual interest, mix materials—glass tiles with stone, ceramic subway tiles with stainless steel.

- Create a finished look by putting an edging detail on top of the backsplash.

- Create drama: let the backsplash extend to the ceiling if there are no upper cabinets.

- Splurge on luxury materials too pricey to use elsewhere.

Edging

Visible edges of countertops need to be finished in some way. The most visually successful choices reflect decorative themes found elsewhere in the kitchen.

A *self-edge* (one made of the same material as the countertop) suits surfaces like natural or engineered stone, solid surface, Richlite, wood, plastic laminate, and tile. The drawings below show the most common self-edges. Square edges are usually the least expensive, but you may want rounded corners for safety. More complex profiles, like full bullnose or ogee, are elegant—but also cost more.

An *applied edge*, like a band of wood or stainless steel, can be used for plastic laminate or tile. Decorative trim tiles and borders are an option for ceramic tile.

The edges of wood countertops or a wood edge applied to another material can be milled into any shape to match other architectural trim in the room. Stone edges are almost as versatile.   ▶▶

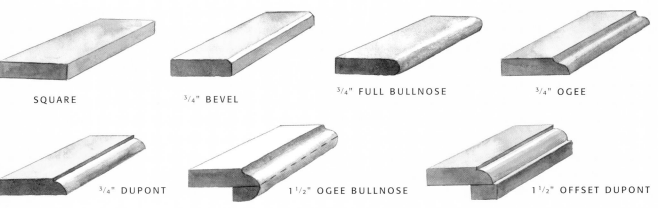

SQUARE   3/4" BEVEL   3/4" FULL BULLNOSE   3/4" OGEE

3/4" DUPONT   1 1/2" OGEE BULLNOSE   1 1/2" OFFSET DUPONT

Comparing Countertops

Concrete

Pros: A natural product available in many colors; heat resistant; can be customized with embedded objects; offers integral sink and drainboard capability; smooth.

Cons: Can develop cracks; needs to be sealed, and the sealer can be damaged by heat and knives; experienced fabricators hard to find.

Engineered stone

Pros: A natural product that resembles stone; offers many patterns and colors; strong; stain and heat resistant; hard to scratch; nonporous (no need to seal) and hygienic (very safe for food preparation).

Cons: Expensive.

Natural stone

Pros: Beautiful natural material in a range of types (granite, marble, limestone, soapstone, slate, lava stone); long lasting; has enduring appeal; heat- and waterproof.

Cons: Solid slabs are expensive, stone tiles a less costly alternative; tends to stain (slate is the most stain resistant) and must be sealed for stain resistance; food acids etch marble.

Plastic laminate

Pros: Inexpensive; comes in lots of colors, patterns, and textures; easy to clean and maintain; stain resistant.

Cons: Has visible seams; heat will damage; burns, stains, and deep scratches can't be repaired.

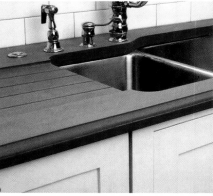

Richlite

Pros: Environmentally friendly product derived from sustainable forests; has natural look like wood; develops natural patina with age; can span considerable lengths without support; heat resistant to 350 degrees.

Cons: Needs sealing for stain resistance; limited colors; UV rays will darken colors; scratches buff out, but not deep cuts.

Solid surface

Pros: Nonporous; tough and low maintenance; resilient; stain resistant; scratches and burns can be sanded; seamless; molds to any shape; allows for integral or undermounted sink.

Cons: Extremely hot items may damage surface; can look artificial compared to real stone.

Contrasting the countertop and the backsplash creates visual interest. Here, blue-flecked granite is a natural foil for the blue and black glass tiles arranged in a patchwork pattern.

Stainless steel

Pros: Durable; waterproof; resistant to bacteria, heat, and stains; integral sink capability; offers commercial look.

Cons: Cold to touch and noisy; will dent and scratch and is then hard to repair; cutting on it damages both countertop and knife; shows water and grease marks if not properly cleaned and dried.

Tile

Pros: Durable; heat resistant; many colors, patterns, and materials; stone tiles provide a less expensive alternative to costly stone slabs.

Cons: Grout (except epoxy) needs sealing (as do some tiles) and can stain or crack; some tile can chip or crack (ceramic) or get etched by acids (marble); not good for rolling dough.

Wood

Pros: A natural product that complements any other material; warm to eye and touch; resilient; scratches and stains can be sanded; hardwood good as cutting surface.

Cons: Porous, thus harder to maintain than nonporous surfaces; requires regular cleaning and sealing or waxing; limited heat resistance.

flooring

Kitchen floors take a lot of wear and tear and require frequent cleaning, so you'll want to give durability and moisture resistance top priority. Comfort underfoot is important, too. But don't feel guilty if looks are what you fall for first—who can resist wood's warmth and natural beauty? Just be sure to weigh the pros and cons of each flooring material before you decide what's right for your kitchen.

Floor show

There are both aesthetic and practical points to keep in mind as you con-sider different flooring possibilities. To see which materials deliver the goods, start by considering the following questions, then consult the chart on the facing page.

Does a flooring material flatter your other kitchen components, like the cabinetry and countertops? Do you prefer a natural material or a manmade one? Is an occasional mopping-up your idea of mainte-nance, or are you up to more demanding care? Will kids and pets be in constant motion in your kitchen, demanding a floor that's extra durable?

Safety is always an issue. Do you need a floor that's slip resistant, for kids and seniors?

Underfoot notes

Here are a few tips to help you through the process of selecting your kitchen flooring. No matter which type of flooring you choose, plan to vacuum or sweep your kitchen often to remove grit brought in by shoes or pets. These micro particles can scratch any floor.

- Don't feel compelled to limit your flooring to a single material. Take a tip from restaurant kitchens: install low-maintenance flooring by the sink and dishwasher—tile or linoleum makes a good choice—and put more glamorous wood or stone where it isn't subject to so much wear and tear.

- Use durable finishes and sealants to toughen high-maintenance flooring materials.

- Soften hard surfaces like stone or tile with runners or area rugs. (Wall-to-wall carpeting, on the other hand, is not a practical option in kitchens—there's just too much mess to contend with.)

Shop Talk

Engineered-wood flooring Layers of base wood cross-stacked for stability, with a veneer top layer of your choice of wood.

Floating installation The joining of planks to one another rather than to a sub-floor—an option for engineered-wood, laminate, and cork floors.

Laminate flooring A photograph of a natural material—often wood—sandwiched between a protective wear coat and a sturdy core. Pergo is one well-known brand.

Reclaimed (recycled) wood Boards salvaged from old buildings or river bot-toms, prized as flooring for their great character and patina. Typical reclaimed species include chestnut, cherry, oak, and heart pine.

Resilient flooring Flexible flooring that has a bit of give. Materials include lino-leum, cork, and vinyl, usually available in either tile or sheet form.

Solid wood Any flooring that is a single piece of wood from top to bottom.

Subflooring What's underneath the surface you walk on. Most floors are attached to a subfloor.

Comparing Flooring

Bamboo

Pros: A sustainable, renewable material; can be more durable than maple or oak; rarely shrinks or expands, unlike other hardwood floors; attractive subtle mottled texture and natural creamy tan or dark caramel color.

Cons: Expensive; distinctive pattern limits use (looks best in contemporary settings).

Ceramic and porcelain tile

Pros: Durable, easy to maintain, stain resistant if sealed or glazed; many colors and patterns; inexpensive to moderate cost (porcelain is the most expensive).

Cons: Can be cold, ungiving underfoot, noisy, and, if glazed, slippery; porous tiles harbor bacteria and stain; grout needs sealing and can stain; can chip or crack over time.

Concrete

Pros: Offers industrial look for home kitchens; highly durable; accepts colors and embedded or stamped patterns; cleans easily with a damp mop.

Cons: Requires an experienced residential installer; must be sealed and may need resealing in high-traffic areas; cold and hard underfoot; moderate to high cost.

Hardwood

Pros: Natural material with a warm appearance; comfortable to walk on; can be refinished; low-maintenance if sealed; expanding choices like cherry, mahogany, and walnut along with oak, maple, and birch.

Cons: Scratches and dents; moisture between boards can cause warping; requires occasional light sanding and resealing to renew, refinishing to restore; moderate to high cost.

Laminate

Pros: Wood or stone look-alike; very tough—resists abuse, from dents and pet scratches to burns and stains; good for high-traffic zones; easy to install.

Cons: Lacks random visual textures of real wood; susceptible to water damage; can't be refinished; moderate to high cost.

Resilient

Pros: Cushiony underfoot; durable; improved protective finishes resist moisture and stains; easy to install and maintain; mutes noise; available as sheets or versatile tiles; lots of colors and patterns; relatively modest cost.

Cons: Vulnerable to dents and tears; moisture may collect between seams if improperly installed.

Stone

Pro: Beautiful natural material—slate, marble, granite, limestone; many color choices; durable; easy to maintain if sealed.

Cons: Requires a strong, well-supported subfloor; cold and hard underfoot; slippery if polished (marble); grout and more porous types (limestone) can stain; needs periodic sealing; expensive.

Lighting *Guidelines*

A SINGLE CEILING-MOUNTED FIXTURE, once a kitchen mainstay, isn't sufficient for today's busy kitchens. The key to good lighting is choosing bulbs and fixtures that support your kitchen's main activities, then placing them in exactly the right spots. Working in poor light is both visually fatiguing and frustrating: if you can't see into a drawer clearly, how can you find what you need?

Creating a lighting plan

Good lighting is the result of a customized scheme that layers carefully selected fixtures and types of lighting. Designers separate lighting into three categories: task, ambient, and accent. All of them contribute to the overall visual warmth that light gives a room.

Strong, focused task lighting illuminates a particular area where an activity—such as measuring baking ingredients—takes place. Ambient or general lighting provides overall illumination, filling in the shadows with a soft level of light—enough, say, for munching a midnight snack. Accent lighting, which is primarily decorative, is used to highlight architectural features or displays, to set a mood, or to provide drama.

A visit to a lighting showroom is a good first step toward coming up with a successful lighting plan. Try to find one that's set up with many sample fixtures and a variety of

Left: Hidden under-cabinet task lighting doubles here as accent light, showcasing a glass-mosaic backsplash. At night, it provides a soft ambient glow.

lighting controls. That way you can experience a range of bulbs, see how light interacts with different surfaces, and decide which kind of light looks best to your eye. Be sure to bring along your floor plan.

Switches and dimmers

Lighting controls give your lighting plan flexibility and finesse. Here are some setup options to consider.

Switches let you fine-tune layers of lighting. You can cluster several lights on one switch—those over the sink and countertops, for example. Separate switches might control the light over the island or the room's main ambient lighting. You can control lights from two locations, like the opposite ends of the kitchen.

Think about dedicating a separate switch for "fill-in" or "in-and-out" light. This could be the pendants over the sink or the strip fixture under the cabinets. Rather than illuminating the whole kitchen, you'll get just enough light to grab a drink of water or open the refrigerator.

With a dimmer, you can alter the mood by changing the amount of light: cheerful at breakfast, low-key for dining.

Top right: This wide-open space benefits from layers of light: ceiling tracks, low-hanging pendants over the island, and under-cabinet fixtures illuminating the countertops. **Bottom right:** Tiny puck lights illuminate display niches, making good use of hard-to-reach upper cabinets.

light fixtures

Finding the right combination of fixtures can be confusing—the variety of styles and finishes is huge, and growing all the time. And you must factor in the requirements of local electrical codes. How do you decide?

Spotlight on fixtures

A primary consideration when choosing a fixture is how it directs light: narrow and focused (for task or accent lighting), in a broad spread (for general or decorative lighting), or somewhere in between. Determine what you need in your kitchen and match those requirements to fixture beam patterns. Consider, too, how easy it is to clean a fixture and to replace bulbs. Another factor: everyone sees light differently. Take advantage of working displays at lighting showrooms to learn which fixtures and bulbs look right to you.

TRIM RINGS

Recessed downlights

Small and discreet, recessed downlights are the most popular choice for kitchens because they can handle the gamut of lighting challenges—general illumination as well as task light for particular activities. (In most kitchens, you'll want other sources, too, at least to fill in the shadows.) Configure them to your needs with modular accessories: baffles, lenses, and louvers to shape light; trim rings to cover the rough edges of the fixture housing and ceiling hole. You can even update existing fixtures by switching your current trims for a new style or finish.

Puck lights are mini recessed fixtures. Use them to light display cabinets or niches, mount them under cabinets to brighten work areas, or install them above cabinets to subtly wash upper walls with light.

Left: Recessed and ceiling-mounted fixtures supplement natural daylight and create a light-filled space at night.

PENDANT FIXTURE

Surface mounts

Fixtures installed on walls or ceilings are excellent at providing general lighting. Some are highly decorative, too. A small chandelier hung over the breakfast table adds sparkle and a touch of formality. A run of ultra-modern pendants above an island offers eye-catching task lighting. If a pendant is used over a table, be sure the shade is narrow enough to hang safely away from diners' heads.

Track lighting

For versatility and installation ease, you can't beat track fixtures. Easy to add to, easy to aim, they provide general, task, and accent lighting in one flexible system. Tracks accept individual fixtures that swivel and move, directing light just where you need it. They're a popular alternative to recessed downlights if you can't or don't want to poke holes in the ceiling.

Shop Talk

Dimmers Wall-mounted controls that take the place of light switches, enabling you to set a fixture at any level from a soft glow to a radiant brightness.

Fluorescent light Steady, shadowless illumination produced when mercury vapor burning inside a tube is reradiated by a phosphor coating. Unrivaled for energy efficiency, fluorescent tubes last far longer than incandescent bulbs. In some areas, general lighting for new kitchens must be fluorescent. (See "Fluorescent Facts," page 65.)

Incandescent light The warm glow produced by a tungsten filament burning slowly in a glass bulb. The pear-shaped A bulb is the most familiar type.

Lamp The industry term for a light bulb or tube used in a fixture, not the fixture itself.

Low-voltage lighting Smaller, safer, and more energy-efficient than standard 120-volt systems, using a transformer to step down electrical current from 120V to 12 or 24 volts. Good for accent lighting, track fixtures, and recessed downlights, for either incandescent or halogen bulbs.

Quartz halogen light A bright, white beam produced by a bulb containing halogen gas, excellent for task lighting, pinpoint accenting, and other dramatic effects. Halogen bulbs outshine incandescent sources and last dramatically longer. The down side: they can run very hot (less of a problem than in the past), are costly, and require special fixtures.

Xenon lights Tiny, cooler-burning spin-offs of halogen, with an extra-long life span. They're naturals for strip lights, under-cabinet task fixtures, and recessed display lights as well as hard-to-reach built-in coves and soffits.

For track systems with high-tech style, check out low-hanging cable lights, flexible track lights, and monorail systems.

Under-cabinet fixtures

These thin, narrow task lights fit below upper wall cabinets and shine down on countertops, eliminating shadows and giving off a soft glow in an otherwise unlit kitchen—especially pleasant when you entertain. Fluorescents are popular here, satisfying local codes requiring that the first switch you come to in the kitchen turns on this type of light. Incandescent, halogen, and xenon strips can also be used under cabinets.

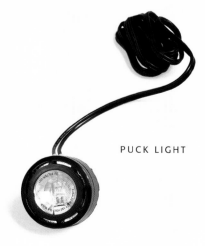

PUCK LIGHT

Remodeling *Realities*

WHAT LURKS BEHIND THE WALLS of your kitchen is often the great unknown, especially if you are remodeling an older home. You'll find out what's there, for better or worse, if you're shifting or adding appliances, installing a vent hood, or removing a wall. On these pages we offer an overview of kitchen systems to prepare you for some basic remodeling realities.

Structural changes

Walls are either bearing (supporting the weight of ceiling joists and/or second-story walls) or nonbearing, as shown in the diagram on the facing page. If you're removing all or part of a bearing wall, you must bridge the gap with a sturdy beam and posts. Nonbearing (partition) walls usually can be removed without too much difficulty—unless pipes or wires are routed through them.

Doors and windows require special framing, as shown; the necessary header size depends on the opening width and local codes. Skylights require similar cuts through ceiling joists and/or rafters. Planning a vaulted or cathedral ceiling? You'll probably need a few beams to maintain structural soundness.

If you opt for a large commercial range or a built-in refrigerator, be sure your floor can support it. You may need to beef up the floor framing to support the extra weight. ▶ ▶

Left: Planning an island? Make sure you can bring electricity to it and connect vent ducts from a hood to an outside wall.

Above: Slender columns above a half-wall do the job of a former load-bearing wall. Shallow cabinets accessed from the other side of the low wall hold kids' books and crafts supplies.

STRUCTURAL FRAMING

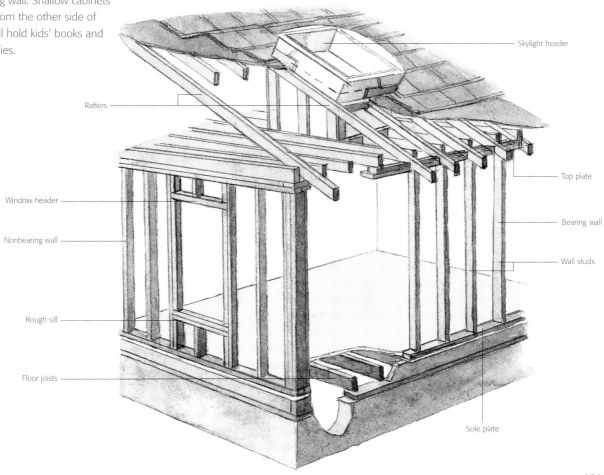

Skylight header

Rafters

Top plate

Window header

Bearing wall

Nonbearing wall

Wall studs

Rough sill

Floor joists

Sole plate

Plumbing concerns

Moving the sink to another location in the kitchen is an easy job—at least conceptually. But if your house has a concrete slab foundation, you'll need to drill through the slab or bring the pipes through the wall from another point above floor level.

Every house has a main soil stack. Below the level of the fixtures, it's your home's primary drainpipe; at its upper end, which protrudes through the roof, the stack becomes a vent. To minimize costs and keep the work simple, plan to situate any new fixture as close as possible to existing pipes. A new fixture within a few feet of the main stack usually can be drained and vented by the stack. But a fixture located far away from the main stack may require its own branch drain and a secondary vent stack—which adds up to a big job. Be sure to check your local plumbing codes for exact requirements.

If your current plumbing line is galvanized pipe, which will corrode over time, you might consider an upgrade to noncorrosive copper, which will last indefinitely. Replacing all your home's plumbing lines may not be an option. But it might make sense in the kitchen if you're already down to the studs for a remodel.

If you are converting from electricity to gas or simply relocating a gas appliance, keep these things in mind:

- The plumbing code (or separate gas code) will specify pipe size (figured according to cubic-foot capacity and the length of pipe between the meter or storage tank and the appliance).

- Any gas appliance that you buy should have a plate stamped with a numerical rating in BTUs per hour.

- Each gas appliance needs to have a nearby code-approved shut-off valve with a straight handle so gas can be turned off easily in an emergency.

Left: In remodeling, the most economical option is to keep the sink (or a pair of them, as shown here) in its original spot. Moving it elsewhere may not be a difficult task, but it will be more costly.

Electrical updates

When planning your new kitchen, take a good look at the existing electrical system. Especially in an older house, you might not have enough service to supply all those sleek new appliances. Be prepared to add circuits—three to five for the typical kitchen makeover.

The National Electrical Code (NEC) requires that all kitchen receptacles be protected by ground fault circuit interrupters (GFCIs) that cut off

Left: By code, every major appliance, including the refrigerator, must have a separate dedicated circuit. Remodeling an older kitchen may require adding circuits.

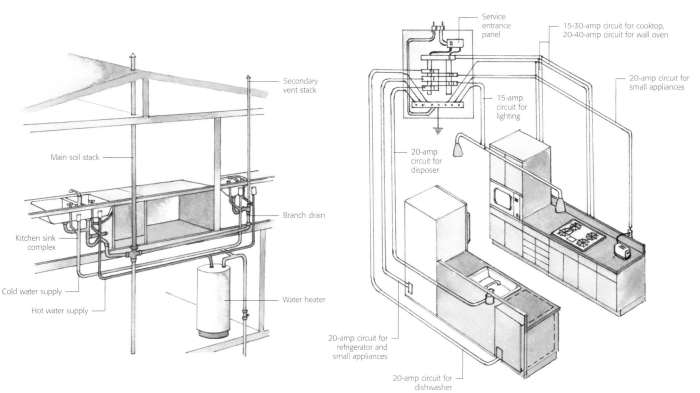

PLUMBING PIPES

Secondary vent stack

Main soil stack

Branch drain

Kitchen sink complex

Cold water supply

Hot water supply

Water heater

ELECTRICAL WIRING

Service entrance panel

15-30-amp circuit for cooktop, 20-40-amp circuit for wall oven

20-amp circuit for small appliances

15-amp circuit for lighting

20-amp circuit for disposer

20-amp circuit for refrigerator and small appliances

20-amp circuit for dishwasher

power immediately if current begins to leak anywhere along the circuit. Other NEC requirements:

- Plug-in outlets and switches for small appliances and the refrigerator must be served by a minimum of two 20-amp circuits.

- A dedicated circuit is required for each major appliance—stove, wall oven, refrigerator, dishwasher, garbage disposer.

- Any countertop area must be within 2 feet of an outlet (a maximum spacing of 4 feet between countertop outlets).

- An island or peninsula must have at least one receptacle.

HVAC systems

Heating, ventilation, and air-conditioning hardware—lumped together as HVAC systems—may all be affected by your proposed kitchen remodel. Your local plumbing codes or a separate mechanical code may dictate the changes you can or are required to make.

Air-conditioning and heating ducts are relatively easy to reroute if you can gain access from a basement, crawl space, garage wall, or unfinished attic. Radiant-heat pipes or other slab-embedded systems may pose

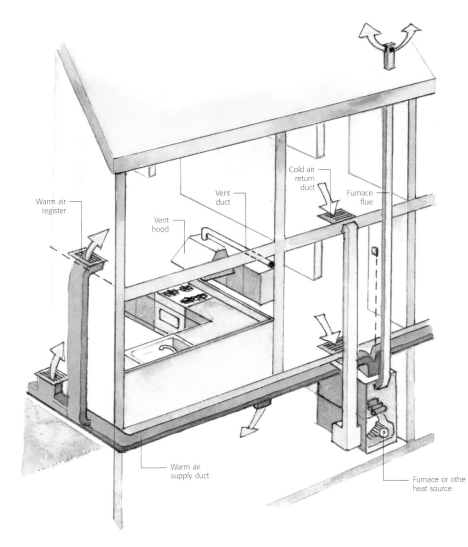

Warm air register

Vent hood

Vent duct

Cold air return duct

Furnace flue

Warm air supply duct

Furnace or other heat source

more of a problem. Registers are usually easy to reposition; the toe space of base cabinets is a favorite spot for retrofits. Don't locate any cold air returns in the new kitchen.

You'll need ventilation for any new freestanding range, cooktop, or wall oven—a hood above or a downdraft system exiting through the floor or

an exterior wall (see pages 136–137). Be sure you will be able to run ductwork for ventilation to the outside of the house if you are changing the location of any of these appliances.

SETTING UP
a Temporary Kitchen

You think you'll survive on take-out dinners, but weeks into a remodel, even a makeshift kitchen begins to look better than none at all. And if you have kids at home, a temporary area for meal prep and eating is a must.

Your strategy depends on how long you will be out of your kitchen and how much you want to spend in the interim. The issues are the same as with a real kitchen: where to store things, prepare meals, eat, clean up. You'll miss your sink most of all—the bathroom is the usual fallback choice. Here are some suggestions to help you get by until your new space is ready.

- Prepare and freeze microwavable meals in advance.

- Move your current refrigerator into a dining area or nearby space (unless you have a second fridge elsewhere).

- If a source of water and a drain are nearby and accessible (in a laundry room, for example), your contractor could hook up an inexpensive utility sink, available at home centers.

- Set up a microwave oven, a toaster oven, and an electric coffee maker on a large and sturdy folding table. Weather permitting, a grill outdoors is a lifesaver (never use a charcoal grill indoors).

- Now is the time to dig out that slow cooker from storage. Requiring no ventilation and minimal attention from the cook, it's the perfect appliance for a household without a stove or an oven.

- Check with your contractor or electrician about potential circuit overloads in your temporary kitchen space. You could lose power if you run a microwave and toaster oven simultaneously, for example. You might need to spread out demand by running extension cords to other circuits.

- Create a work surface and some storage space with a length of plywood set on a pair of your old base cabinets.

- Buy lots of disposable dinnerware—lots!

You're going to be living without a functioning kitchen for weeks or months. How will you cope? All will go more smoothly if you plan for a temporary kitchen along with your new one.

ventilation

Installing a kitchen without planning for proper ventilation is akin to lighting a fire in the fireplace without opening the damper. You need to remove the smoke, heat, grease, moisture, and odors produced by cooking. The system you choose should effectively tackle all that while making as little noise as possible. These days, looks really count, too. You'll find that today's vent hoods reflect current trends in materials, from industrial-look stainless steel to dramatic ultra-contemporary glass.

Shop Talk

Capture The ability of a hood's canopy to grab or "capture" grease vapors, heat, odor, and moisture.

Cubic feet per minute (CFM) A rating of a vent system's power—how much air is moved, and how fast; the higher the number, the greater the exhaust flow.

Sones A measure of noise level; the lower the number, the quieter the system.

Designer-sleek, they can be the focal point of a kitchen design.

Clearing the air

The best vent hoods work by grabbing air (the "capture"), forcing it through a filter, and then exhausting it to the outdoors through a duct. Recirculating ductless hoods are an alternative if exterior venting is not an option. These draw out some smoke and grease through charcoal filters before returning the air back into the room.

The design and layout of your kitchen, along with local building codes, will dictate your choice. You also may prefer the look of one type over the other. But your main decision is between updraft and downdraft systems.

Left: This minimalist wall hood consists of a stainless-steel "chimney" with glass canopy. Its sleek lines allow a nearly unimpeded view of the counter-to-ceiling glass-tile backsplash.

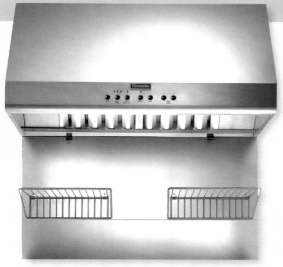

UPDRAFT WITH OPTIONAL BACKSPLASH

DOWNDRAFT WITH SMOOTHTOP ELECTRIC COOKTOP

Updraft. Installed above the cooktop to draw air up and out, a hood canopy may be one of two styles. *Cabinet/wall-mount* metal hood canopies mount beneath overhead cabinetry (ducts are hidden), while *chimney* types are wall-mounted or hung over an island, with a canopy (usually metal, but glass is a designer option) attached to a chimney-shaped metal duct cover.

Downdraft. Best for an open-plan kitchen with a cooktop in an island or peninsula, downdraft vent units are built into a base cabinet or are part of the cooktop itself. They use air currents to draw smoke, heat, and moisture downward; grease is trapped below. This type is good at moving air, less effective at capturing smoke or odors rising from tall pots. *Telescoping* units store below the work surface, rising at the push of a button when needed; *center* units hide behind grillwork set between cooktop modules.

What do you need?

Get the model with the most airflow (CFM), best capture, and least noise that you can afford. Commercial-style ranges and cooktops, which can really crank out the heat, usually require higher-end ventilation systems. Consult product specifications for your cooktop and ask for help at appliance stores.

Power (CFM). Be sure the system you buy is up to the job you need it to do. For today's efficient residential cooktops, 300 CFM is usually the minimum recommended rating. Commercial-style models demand 600 to 1,000 CFM or higher. Check the cooktop manufacturer's recommendations for your setup.

Size. A hood should cover the entire cooking area. Install a standard hood so its bottom is 18 to 24 inches above the surface of a residential-style cooktop. Install more powerful pro-style hoods 24 to 30 inches above the cooking surface, or as the manufacturer directs.

Accessories. Possible add-ons include utensil bars, decorative rails, a restaurant-style heat lamp, and a backsplash with racks. Hood liners let you fit a vent inside a custom decorative shell.

Filter Tips

A clean filter enhances vent performance. Removable mesh filters and baffle filters (V-shaped bars offered with some pro-style systems) are dishwasher safe. Clean mesh filters monthly and baffle filters as needed, depending on how often you cook and how much grease you generate; replace charcoal filters from ductless units every 3 to 6 months. Some models have a light that goes on when filters need cleaning. To avoid the issue altogether, install one of the new filterless systems; grease gets deposited into cups that you lift out for disposal.

Putting It
All Together

YOU'VE WORKED OUT AN EFFICIENT LAYOUT, chosen appliances, organized storage, and decided on style, lighting, and color. The last step is a revised floor plan. Finalize your choice of countertop and flooring materials and start thinking about furnishings and all those little things with big design impact—doorknobs and drawer pulls, hinges and moldings, even window latches.

The final plan

To discover which codes may affect your project and whether a permit is required, check with your city or county building department. If you do need a permit, the building department will require an accurate and detailed floor plan, or working drawing. Even if you don't need a permit, your project will go more smoothly if you've drawn it all out carefully.

Create your final floor plan the way you did your original scale plan (see page 79), trans-ferring to the new plan all the features you want to preserve and adding the changes you wish to make. If you prefer, you can hire a designer, drafter, or contractor to draw the final plan for you. Elevation sketches (see page 109) aren't usually required, but they'll prove helpful for planning the work. ▶▶

Left: Cabinets are a high-ticket item in a remodel, especially if they are custom built with top-of-the-line details and finishes. Shop around before making a final decision.

NEED HELP
from a Pro?

Be realistic when assessing what you can handle yourself. If you decide to go with outside help, the following are the kinds of professionals you might use. When choosing, consider the cost but don't just look at the numbers—quality of work, reliability, personal rapport, and on-time performance are also important. Ask for the names of recent clients and talk with several to see if they were happy with the process and the results; you might ask to visit the finished site, if possible.

Architects are state-licensed professionals with degrees in architecture. Trained to create designs that are structurally sound, functional, and aesthetically pleasing, they know construction materials, can negotiate contractors' bids, and can supervise the actual work. Many are members of the American Institute of Architects (AIA). If structural calculations must be made, architects can make them; other professionals need state-licensed engineers to design structures and sign working drawings. Architects who don't specialize in kitchens may not be totally familiar with the latest in kitchen design and materials.

General contractors specialize in construction, though some have design skills as well. They may do all the work themselves or assume responsibility for hiring qualified subcontractors, ordering materials, and seeing that the job is completed according to contract. Contractors can secure building permits and arrange for inspection as work progresses.

Interior designers specialize in decorating and furnishing rooms and can offer innovative ideas and advice. Through their contacts, a homeowner has access to materials and products not available at the retail level. If you're working with an architect or kitchen designer, you may still wish to use an interior designer for finishing touches. Some offer complete remodeling services. Many belong to the American Society of Interior Designers (ASID).

Kitchen designers know the hottest trends in cabinets and appliances. However, they may lack the structural knowledge of the architect or the aesthetic skill of a good interior designer. If you decide to work with a kitchen designer, look for a member of the National Kitchen & Bath Association (NKBA). The association has established codes and sponsors programs to inform its members about the latest materials and techniques.

Retail specialists include showroom personnel and building-center staff. If your kitchen requires only a minor face-lift, this may be all the help you need. If you're tackling a larger job, check the specialist's qualifications carefully; some are quite qualified and genuinely helpful, while others may be motivated simply to sell you more goods.

For complicated projects, your building department may also require detailed drawings of structural, plumbing, and wiring changes. You may need to show areas adjacent to the kitchen so officials can tell how the project will affect the rest of your house.

Dollars and cents

The reality check: how much will your new kitchen cost? According to one national industry survey, the average amount spent on a mid-level job is around $42,000. Of course, this is only the sketchiest of estimates. Keep in mind that such averages don't necessarily reflect local variables in material and labor costs, overheads, and margins.

Factors that influence cost include the project size and scope and the finishes you choose. Obviously, if you stick to simple changes—replacing countertops, adding recessed downlights, refacing your cabinets, or replacing a worn-out range—you can hold down costs. On the other hand, extensive structural changes coupled with ultra-high-end materials and appliances can easily propel the amount up into the stratosphere.

Cabinets typically eat up the largest percentage of a budget pie, closely followed by labor, then countertops and appliances. Structural, plumbing,

Above: This handsome kitchen meets all the basic requirements: plenty of work space, well-chosen appliances and materials, and lots of style.

Left: Be realistic with yourself and your designer about budget. You'll spend more if your plans involve an extensive remodel with high-end materials and fixtures.

and electrical changes all affect the final figure significantly.

How do you keep the budget under control? For starters, identify whether you're looking at a simple face-lift, a more extensive replacement, or a major structural remodel. Cabinet, appliance, and material prices vary dramatically. Obtain ballpark figures in different price categories, mull them over, and then present your architect, designer, or retailer with a range of options and a bottom line with which you are comfortable. Of course, you can save a substantial piece of the pie by providing labor yourself—but be sure you're up to the task.

If you use a design professional, expect to be charged either a flat fee or a percentage (usually 10 to 15 percent) of the cost of goods purchased. General contractors include their fees in their bids.

KITCHEN
Remodel Workflow

Depending on the scope of your makeover, the materials you have selected, and contractor preference, your project may not follow these steps exactly. But this list represents a typical job sequence for a kitchen remodel.

Removal

1. Contents of cabinets, drawers, shelves, closets; furniture; objects on countertops; wall decor

2. Appliances

3. Demolition—removal of light fixtures, wallpaper, cabinets, etc. (after sealing off openings to adjacent rooms to control dust and dirt)

Reconstruction

1. Framing for structural changes: walls, doors, windows, skylights

2. Rough plumbing changes

3. Heating and ventilation ducting changes

4. Electrical wiring: outlets, lighting, appliances, telephones

5. Insulation

6. Wall and ceiling coverings

6. Cabinets

7. Templates for fabricating countertops

8. Flooring

9. Finish carpentry: molding, casing, baseboards

10. Paint

11. Countertops and sink

12. Tile (backsplash)

13. Appliances

14. Final touch-ups

Below: A remodel is a messy job. Confine dust and dirt to the work area, if possible, by sealing doorways with plastic sheeting.

If your kitchen remodel is a do-it-yourself project, the list here can help you plan the order of tasks involved in dismantling the old space and installing the new. If you are hiring a contractor, you'll find it useful to know what to expect.

Design and Photography Credits

DESIGN

Ideas and Inspiration

6 Robert Glazier, Hill Glazier Architects, www.hillglazier.com 7BL Architect: Mark Maresca 7BR Jerome Buttrick, Buttrick Wong Architects, www.buttrickwong.com 8 Kitchen design: David Huisman, Chalon US, www.chalonus.com; interior design: Mauvianne Giusti, Bella Villa Designs 9T HhLodesign, www.hhlodesign.com 9B Dan and Lanny Danenberg, Kitchens by Design, www.danenbergdesigns.com; Laurie Ghielmetti Interiors, www.lghielmetti@sigprop.com 10T Gary Milici, Coast Line Construction 10B Sant Architects 11T Kitchen design: David Huisman, Chalon US, www.chalonus.com; interior design: Suzanne Warrick 11B Dan and Lanny Danenberg, Kitchens by Design, www.danenbergdesigns.com 12 Lisa Joyce Architecture, www.lisajoyce@sbcglobal.net; Peter Kyle, Woodworks Construction & Design, www.pkyle@sbcglobal.net 13T Architect: Fran Halperin, Halperin & Christ; interior design: Sharon Low 13B Laurie Ghielmetti and Douglas McDonald, Laurie Ghielmetti Interiors, lghielmetti@sigprop.com 14T Tom Thacher, Thacher & Thompson Architects; interior design: Lorri Kershner, L. Kershner Design, www.lkershnerdesign.com 14CL and B Interior design: Kathleen Navarra, Navarra Design, www.navarradesign.com 15 EDI Architecture; interior design: Pamela Pennington Studios 16 Dan and Lanny Danenberg, Kitchens by Design, www.danenbergdesigns.com 17T Lisa Joyce Architecture, www.lisajoyce@sbcglobal.net; Jonathan Straley Designs; Peter Kyle, Woodworks Construction & Design, www.pkyle@sbcglobal.net 17B Architect: Halperin & Christ; kitchen and rug design: Alicia Keshishian, www.acarpets.com 18 Architect: William Rawn Associates; interior design: Kimberly Nunn and Dan Worden,

Shopworks 19T Eugenia Erskine Jesberg, EJ Interior Design, www.ejinteriordesign.com 19B Architect: Endres Ware; design: Manuela King 20 (main) Architect: Fran Halperin, Halperin & Christ; interior design: Sharon Low 20T Interior design: Kathleen Navarra, Navarra Design, www.navarradesign.com 21TR Jerome Buttrick, Buttrick Wong Architects, www.buttrickwong.com 21L Color consultant: Gail McCabe Designs 21BR Mercedes Corbell Design + Architecture 22T Architect: Malcolm Davis 22B Architect: Patrick Finnegan; Lisa Staprans Interior Design; contractor: Marrone & Marrone 23T Architect: Malcolm Davis 23B David Michael Miller 24 Peter Brock Architect, www.peter-brock.com; cabinets: Peter Witte; contractor: Santilli & Forster 25 Cathy Macfee 27 Cydney Posner 28–29 Architect: David Coleman 30T Interior design: Kendall Agins Design 30B Brad Dunning 31 Christine Curry Designs 32T Dan and Lanny Danenberg, Kitchens by Design, www.danenbergdesigns.com 32B P. Vincent 34B Laurie Ghielmetti and Douglas McDonald, Laurie Ghielmetti Interiors, www.lghielmetti@sigprop.com 35 Lisa Joyce Architecture, www.lisajoyce@sbcglobal.net; Peter Kyle, Woodworks Construction & Design, www.pkyle@sbcglobal.net 36TR Jim O'Neill/OZ Architects 36BR Interior consultant: Peggy Mussafer 37 Peter Brock Architect, www.peter-brock.com; cabinets: Peter Witte; contractor: Santilli & Forster 38 Kitchen design: David Huisman, Chalon US, www.chalonus.com; interior design: Mauvianne Giusti, Bella Villa Designs 39 Lydia Corser, CKD, EcoInteriors; contractor: Brian Corser, Corser Home Services 40 Peter Kyle, Woodworks Construction & Design, www.pkyle@sbcglobal.net 41T Interior design: Lorri Kershner, L. Kershner Design, www.lkershnerdesign.com 41B James Miller, AIA, Oculus Architecture and Design 42 Phillip Sides 43T Nicholas Budd Dutton

Architects 43B Byron Kuth and Elizabeth Ranieri, Kuth/Ranieri Architects 44TL and TR Peter Brock Architect, www.peter-brock.com; cabinets: Peter Witte; contractor: Santilli & Forster 44B Interior consultant: Peggy Mussafer 45 Scott Johnson 46T Jerome Buttrick, Buttrick Wong Architects, www.buttrickwong.com 46B Architect: Endres Ware; design: Manuela King 47T Dan and Lanny Danenberg, Kitchens by Design, www.danenbergdesigns.com 47BL Laurie Ghielmetti and Douglas McDonald, Laurie Ghielmetti Interiors, www.lghielmetti@sigprop.com 47BR Kitchen Matrix, Inc. 48 Architect: Kathryn A. Rogers, Sogno Design Group 49B Laurie Ghielmetti and Douglas McDonald, Laurie Ghielmetti Interiors, www.lghielmetti@sigprop.com 50TR Nancy and Ed Hillner, Kitchen Classics 50BR Beth Gensemer 51 Architect: Dale Gardon; design: Tamm Jasper Interiors 52T Fox Design Group, Architects, www.foxdesigngroup.com; design: Francesca Peck 53 Jeffrey L. Day, Min/Day, with Marc Toma and Lisa K. Trujillo, BurksToma Architects; Marie Fisher and Alissa Lillie, Marie Fisher Interior Design 54 Design and construction: Clark Interiors 55TL Annette Starkey, CKD 55BL Dan and Lanny Danenberg, Kitchens by Design, www.danenbergdesigns.com; Laurie Ghielmetti Interiors, www.lghielmetti@sigprop.com 55R David S. Gast & Associates, Architects, www.dsga.com; Mary Lou D'Auray Interior Design; glass: Smoke & Mirrors, LLC, www.smokeandmirrorsllc.com 56T Ted Flato, Craig McMahon, Jonathan Card, Lake/Flato Architects, Inc.; Susan Lovelace and Patricia Kramer, Lovelace Interiors 56BL and BR Bill Allison, AIA, Steve Hand, Allison Ramsey Architects; Michael Steiner, ASID, and Tim Schelfe, ASID, Steiner + Schelfe Design 57 Architect: Dan Preston; design: Walter Martin, Jr., and Amanda Moon 58T Hershon Hartley Design Group 59T Architect: Patrick

Finnegan; Lisa Staprans Interior Design; contractor: Marrone & Marrone **60T** Tom Thacher, Thacher & Thompson, Architects; Lorri Kershner, L. Kershner Design, www.lkershnerdesign.com; handblown vessels: Kanik Chung, www.kanik glassblowing.com **60B** Francisco Kripacz **61** Architect: Eric Trabert & Associates; Annie Speck Interior Designs; construction: Mulvaney & Co. **62T** Grey Design Studio, www.greydesignstudio.com **62B** Tish Key Interior Design **64** Fox Design Group, Architects, www.foxdesigngroup.com **65T** David S. Gast & Associates, Architects, www.dsga.com; Mary Lou D'Auray Interior Design; glass: Smoke & Mirrors, LLC, www.smokeandmirrorsllc.com **65BL** David Coleman/Architecture, www.davidcoleman .com **65BR** Patrick Tighe, Tighe Architecture; TSO Construction **66TL** John Jennings and Sasha Tarnopolsky, Dry Design **66BL** Lisa Joyce Architecture, www.lisajoyce@sbcglobal. net; Peter Kyle, Woodworks Construction & Design, www.pkyle@sbcglobal.net; Jonathan Straley Designs **66R** Architect: Endres Ware; design: Manuela King **67** Philip Volkmann, Barry & Volkmann Architects, www.bvarchitects.com **68** Marcy Voyevod Interior Design; Keith Construction; cabinets: Tom Diedrich **69B** Lisa Joyce Architecture, www.lisajoyce@sbcglobal.net; Peter Kyle, Woodworks Construction & Design, www.pkyle@sbcglobal.net; Jonathan Straley Designs **70** Kitchen design: David Huisman, Chalon US, www.chalonus.com; interior design: Suzanne Warrick **71TL** Lydia Corser, CKD, EcoInteriors; contractor: Brian Corser, Corser Home Services **71BL** Halperin & Christ, Architects; design: Alicia D. Keshishian **71BR** Interior design: Pamela Pennington **72TL and TR** Cydney Posner **72BR** Interior design: Kathleen Navarra, Navarra Design, Inc., www.navarradesign.com **73T** Design and construction: Harrell Remodeling Design + Build, www.harrell-remodeling.com **73B** Dan and Lanny Danenberg, Kitchens by Design, www.danenbergdesigns.com **74** Philip Volkmann/Barry & Volkmann Architects, www.bvarchitects.com **75T** Lydia Corser, CKD, EcoInteriors; contractor: Brian Corser, Corser Home Services **75B** Kitchen design: David Huisman, Chalon US, www.chalonus.com; interior design: Suzanne Warrick

How to Do It

76 Dirk Stennick, Architect **77L** J. Stephen Peterson & Associates **77R** Kitchen design: David Huisman, Chalon US, www.chalonus.com; interior design: Suzanne Warrick **79** Brukoff Design Associates **80** Peter Breese **83B** Lindy Small Architecture **86** Michael Stein, Stein/Troost Architects **90** Indian Rock Design/Build, www.indianrockdesign.com **92B** Stephen Swearengen Architect; Jon Schmidt Interior Design; construction: Rob Murray, Masterworks **93T** Architect: Karl Golden **96B** Peter Brock Architect, www.peter-brock.com; cabinets: Peter Witte; contractor: Santilli & Forster **100** Indian Rock Design/Build, www.indianrockdesign.com **103** Jerome Buttrick, Buttrick Wong Architects **104B** Architect: Mark Maresca **106TL** Anne Phillips Architecture **107TL** Lindy Small Architecture **108T** Kitchen Matrix, Inc. **108B** Architect: Richard Becker **110BL** Stephen Kanner Architects **111B** Kitchen Matrix, Inc. **112TL** Woodgrain Woodworks **112TR** La Vita è Bella/Scavolini **113T** Pamela Pennington Studios **113B** DeMattei Construction; interior design: Ann Bertelsen and Leanne Holder **114T** Jim Estes, Estes/Twombly Architects **114B** Fox Design Group, Architects, www.foxdesigngroup.com; Navarra Design Inc., www.navarradesign.com **115TR** La Vita è Bella/Scavolini **115CR** Kitchen Matrix, Inc. **116** Buttrick Wong Architects **117T** David S. Gast & Associates, Architects, www.dsga.com; design: Carole White **118B** Terry Martin Associates. A.I.A.; interior design: McDonald & Moore Ltd. **120L** Melody Emerick, Emerick Architects **120R** Butler Amsden Architects **123T** Fox Design Group, Architects, www.foxdesigngroup.com **123BL** Osburn Design **123BM** Harrell Remodeling Design + Build, www. harrell-remodeling.com **125 #1** Ann Knight, TimberGrass **125 #4** David S. Gast & Associates, Architects, www.dsga. com; Mary Lou D'Auray Interior Design **126B** Eugenia Erskine Esberg, EJ Interior Design **127T** Nick Notes Architecture, San Francisco, www.nnarchitecture.com **127B** Architect: Mastro & Skylar **128BL** Bethe Cohen Design Associates **130B** Jon Dick, Archaeo Architects **131** Karen Austin, CKD, Creative Kitchens & Bath **132** Cyndy Cantley **133** Cynthia S. Muni **136** Mercedes Corbell Design + Architecture, www.mercedescorbelldesign.com **140T** Butler Amsden Architects **140B** Jon Dick, Archaeo Architects

PHOTOGRAPHY

Jean Allsopp: 56–57 Scott Atkinson: 126T Rob D. Brodman: 63T Barry Brukoff: 79 James Carrier: 84, 118T Van Chaplin: 7L, 104 Glen Christiansen: 123BL Beatriz Coll: 128B Grey Crawford: 20T, 43T Tria Giovan: 42, 59B, 132 Laurey W. Glenn: 36BR, 44B Jay Graham: 53 John Granen: 28, 29, 65BL, 107TL Art Gray: 18, 65BR Art Grice: 125 #1 Jamie Hadley: 8, 9B, 11–14, 16–17, 19B, 20 main photo, 22B, 24, 30T, 32T, 34–35, 36L, 37, 38–40, 41T, 44, 46B, 47, 49B, 55BL, 58B, 59T, 60T, 66R, 66BL, 69B, 70, 71TL and BL, 72BR, 73B, 75, 77R, 92T, 96B, 108A, 111, 112R, 115, 117B Margot Hartford: 27, 52T, 54, 55TL, 55R, 58T, 64, 65T, 72TL, 72TR, 73T, 76, 78T, 90, 100, 112L, 114B, 117T, 123T, 123CB, 125 #4, 131, 136 Alex Hayden: 9T James Frederick Housel: 77L Ivalo Lighting Inc.: 63B Rob Karosis: 10T, 86, 114T Rick Keating: 120L Muffy Kibbey: 31, 41B, 67, 68, 69T, 71BR, 74, 83, 93T, 113B, 118B, 120R, 140T davidduncanlivingston.com: 25, 125 #2 Kathryn MacDonald: 22T, 23T E. Andrew McKinney: 19T, 126B, 128T, 129B Matthew Millman: 92B John O'Hagan: 57 Pamela Pennington Studios: 113T J.D. Peterson: 103, 127T PhotoDisc, Inc.: 139 Heather Reid: 21BR, 48 Lisa Romerein: 10B, 66T Bill Rothschild: 138B Mark Rutherford: 130T Alan Shortall: 125 #7 Michael Skott: 26, 121, 122TR and BL Thomas J. Story: 6, 7R, 15, 21TR and L, 43B, 46T, 50TL, 51, 61, 62, 106T, 116 Tim Street-Porter: 30B, 32B, 45, 60B, 78B, 89, 110BL Brian Vanden Brink: 80 Don Vandervort: 135, 138T, 141 Dominique Vorillon: 23B, 33, 50BR, 71CR, 130B, 140B David Wakely: 36TR Jessie Walker: 50TR, 108B, 127B, 133 Courtesy of: American Standard: 107BL Blum: 109 Bosch: 71TR Crystal Cabinet Works, Inc.: 110 (3) DuPont: 122TM and BR Elmira Stove Works: 99T Fisher & Paykel Appliances: 105T Formica Corp.: 125 #5 KitchenAid Home Appliances: 95, 96T, 99B, 102B Kohler Co.: 107TM and TR, 123BR Miele: 97L, 101 #1 and #2 Moen: 106M and B, 107BR Richlite (photo by Doug Ogle): 122BM Sonoma Cast Stone: 122TL Sub-Zero and Wolf: 49T, 50BL, 52B, 72BL, 93B, 101 #3 and #4 Thermador: 98, 102T, 105B, 137 Viking: 97R Wicanders Cork Flooring: 125 #6

Index

Numbers in **bold type** refer to photo captions.